The TV Director/Interpreter

The TV Director/Interpreter

By COLBY LEWIS

Professor, Television and Radio Department
Michigan State University

ILLUSTRATED BY THE AUTHOR

COMMUNICATION ARTS BOOKS

Hastings House Publishers · New York 10016

791.45
LEW
7/7L

Text Edition SBN: 8038–7041–8
Cloth Edition SBN: 8038–7042–6

Library of Congress Catalog Card Number: 68–27639

Published simultaneously in Canada by
Saunders of Toronto Ltd., Don Mills, Ontario

Printed in the United States of America

Contents

Acknowledgments

This book reflects the contributions of:

A. M. Drummond, fondly remembered Director of the Cornell University Theatre, who gave me my principal education in dramatic and visual communication.

William Strunk, Jr., onetime professor of English at Cornell University, whose course and little book on *The Elements of Style* have helped me not only with writing, but with formulating a "grammar" for television camerawork.

Sprague Vonier, now manager of WTMJ-TV, who, as a fellow director and partner to many stimulating conversations, generated ideas and phrases which he may find surviving here in print.

Nick Brauer, who, as engineering supervisor at WTMJ-TV, helped a neophyte to understand the potentialities and limitations of the television electronic system.

Leo A. Martin, Chairman of the Television and Radio Department at Michigan State University, who encouraged me to return to teaching and write a book.

Faculty colleagues Arthur Weld and Robert Schlater, and WMSB audio supervisor Donald Kemp, who have read parts of the manuscript and provided valuable suggestions.

A. William Bluem, Newhouse Communications Center of Syracuse University, who helped to put the manuscript in good hands.

Lastly, Dr. David Berlo, Chairman of the Communication Department at Michigan State University, whose question "How do you know it's true?" reminds me to caution the reader that most of the principles in this book, although I believe them to be empirically sound, have yet to be scientifically validated. To him, therefore, this book is offered as a hopeful stimulus for many experimental studies.

COLBY LEWIS

East Lansing, Michigan
1968

Introduction

As a televison director you are an interpreter of the program action to its audience. The audience understands the action only as you translate it through the media of your cameras and microphones. To convey to the audience the right sights and the right sounds at the right times, in order to affect its members in the manner intended by the program—this is your chief responsibility. To make you fully aware of this responsibility and help you to fulfill it is the purpose of this book.

The book presumes that you are either taking a course in television directing or that, although you may already be directing professionally, you are still studying how to increase your perception of the role and your proficiency at it. It further presumes that you are familiar with the tools, techniques and terminology of television production which must be mastered before starting to learn the director's job.

In this book you will find the product of one man's experience, which includes six years as a director, five years as a supervisor of other directors in both commercial and educational stations, and another five years as teacher of a course in directing at a university.

From that course came the impetus and material for this book. So brief were class meeting times in proportion to what should be learned that most of them were consumed, not by absorbing principles of communication, but by getting accustomed to briefing crews and talent, calling shots, watching monitors and bringing the show off on schedule. In order to let the students have maximum opportunity to learn by doing, the instructor minimized his verbal comments in favor of "handouts" to be read outside of class. A compilation of these handouts evolved into the present book. Possibly some other instructor, faced with similar circumstances, may find the text useful for stating what he lacks time to say during class sessions.

Rather than describing professional practices in the detached fashion of some texts in the field, this book tries to talk to you directly, giving you principles which you can put to use. The learning experiences of students who took the author's course are used to make these principles clearer to you.

To help impress the principles upon your mind and make it easier for you to review them quickly, major statements have been given special typographical emphasis. As an intended help to your instructor, the statements have also been numbered. He can cite these numbers to save time and prevent ambiguity whenever he wishes to call specific principles to your attention.

Most of the principles are concerned with visual communication, because working with cameras is likely to take most of a director's time, and because many students may already be familiar with audio communication from courses in radio which preceded those in television. Yet even they may need to review the chapter called "Don't Forget Audio."

All of the principles are collected in Part One, which forms the major portion of the book and constitutes what might be called a kind of "grammar of the camera." Although most of the handouts previously mentioned were used to constitute this grammar, there were others concerned with the development of certain aptitudes (making floorplans, calling shots, and being an efficient administrator) which contribute so much to the success of the director as an interpreter that it seemed unwise to omit them. Therefore, chapters on these aptitudes are included as Part Two.

To make the book useful for as long as possible and under the greatest variety of circumstances, an attempt has been made to stick to principles which apply regardless of the type of equipment you are using. It is impossible, however, to predict what new capabilities will be attained in present equipment or what new equipment will take over in coming years. It does seem likely that color, now adopted for network programming, will also soon dominate local production. Instead of being separated out as something new and special, material about directing for color television will be found within several chapters, supporting various communication principles along with other recommendations which apply equally to color and monochrome.

Since the book had to stop somewhere—and perhaps leave room for a sequel—it is not concerned with the role of the producer or writer. It assumes that the program purpose has already been determined and that the content (what is to be said and done on the program) has already been formulated and is now waiting for you, with cameras and microphones, to interpret it accurately and effectively to your audience.

Chapter 1

Planning Picture Statements

As a director you take pictures of the action which passes before your cameras. But what, of all the things in sight, should a given picture include? And when is it time to change to a different picture? And by what means can you effect this change?

Some answers to these basic and important questions are provided by the picture-planning process which is outlined below:

1 Divide the action of your program into picture statements.

A writer knows that he would be understood only with the greatest difficulty were he to issue an unbroken stream of words. Therefore, he communicates by making one impression at a time. To distinguish these impressions he uses punctuation; he marks off his message to clarify its structure and meaning.

For the same purpose, the director uses what may be called pictorial punctuation. As the writer divides his words into sentences, the director divides the action of his program into picture statements.

1.1   *A picture statement, like a sentence, has a subject.*

This subject is the item (or group of related items) upon which, at a given moment, you train your camera because it is important then. Your picture statement says, "See, these are the two persons who are talking together," or, "This is the thing they are talking about," or, "Notice this man for what he is doing."

The subjects are apt to keep changing, and each new subject requires from you a new picture statement.

1.2   But just as a writer may use the same subject for a series of sentences, a director may maintain the same subject, yet take different pictures of it.

For example, he shows a man at table filling a glass. Then he shows predominantly the man's face, grimacing with the glass at his lips. These statements have the same subject, "man with glass," but different predicates. The first statement predicates that he "is pouring a drink," the second that he "doesn't like the taste of it."

Had the grimace been taken with the same framing as the filling of the glass, it would not have made so distinct an impression. By eliminating the table surface, which was no longer important, and contracting attention to the man's face, which had become all important, the director pointed up the man's reaction to the drink, having decided that this was sufficiently significant to warrant its own special statement.

1.3   There are then two reasons for changing picture statements:

(1) To direct attention to a new subject.

(2) To reveal a new aspect of the same subject in order to emphasize a different point about it.

2   Learn to perceive the program content as a succession of points.

At every moment of the program your picture must say to the audience, "See, this is the point!"

But before you can make your audience see the point, you must first be able to discern it yourself. You must be able to perceive your program content as a succession of changing points.

2.1   Don't wait for a television assignment to practice this discernment.

You can analyze any action which you happen to witness, asking, "What points should I communicate pictorially to make what is happening intelligible to an audience?"

2.2   Example: a science lesson:

See, the instructor is challenging his students to pay close attention to the next demonstration.

See, his demonstration equipment is on the counter.

See, here is the substance with which he is concerned.

See, he is placing the substance on a scale.

See, the indicator on the scale is registering a certain value.

. . . and so on, through various other "see" statements.

2.3   Example: a twirling act:

In the example just given, each new point involves a different subject. Discerning the points is sometimes more difficult but no less important when the subject remains constant. This can be illustrated by a baton twirling act which was put on camera by a student director. His twirler was skillful, but because he showed her stunts in one unchanging full shot, they tended to blur into one another and lose their individual effectiveness.

Then, being challenged to analyze the performance, he came to perceive it as a sequence of distinct accomplishments, each of which could be differentiated and enhanced by its own individual picture treatment. Rolling the baton around the shoulders, he decided, could be made more assertive by a chest shot which would narrow attention to it. Throwing the baton aloft could be dramatized by a full shot from a low camera position which would accentuate the height of the throw. The skill required to spin the baton rapidly could be played up by having the performer walk towards camera until all one saw was vibrating fingers and flashing spokes.

3   By punctuating thus, you gain several advantages:

3.1   You reveal the distinct nature of each point.

To secure this advantage, you cannot make more than one impression at a time.

For example, a program guest is presenting "The Five Rules of Water Safety." As he introduces each rule, he points to a card, shown in closeup, on which all five rules are lettered. But each time he points, other rules on the card compete for attention with the one under consideration, and since the viewers can read ahead of the speaker, they tend to listen to him with impatience.

To circumvent this difficulty one can re-letter the rules one to a card—

or, keeping them all on the same card, one can start with them individually concealed in some fashion and then unmask each at its proper time. Thus, each rule will make its due impression while adding to the ones previously exposed in a cumulative effect.

3.2   *You keep new things happening.*

In the example above, note that first only rule #1 is important, then rule #2 enters the action, then comes the turn of rule #3. Thus, new information keeps occurring.

Television is often cited as a visual medium. It should also be regarded as a temporal one, in which the maintenance of interest requires change and progression. To support this progression a unique advantage is offered by the camera: obviously used to show things, it should also be valued for its ability *not* to show them until their time comes to enter the action.

Another advantage of sequential picture statements, then, is that by showing one thing at a time you can keep new things happening.

This advantage also applies to the twirling act previously cited. As originally put on camera, it tended to grow monotonous without picture changes to point up action changes and to say in effect, "Look, here is something new and different beginning!"

3.3   *You clarify the structure of your material.*

To mark where one unit of the action ends and another begins is important for helping the audience to grasp the structure of the program material. Remember this when analyzing the points in musical material:

> Whole band for the first eight measures.
> Reeds for the second eight.
> Trumpets for the third eight—and so on.

In this instance you are using your picture statements to establish which instruments are playing at a particular time. Your punctuation is also clarifying the musical structure, which is based on figures lasting eight measures.

In like manner, a new picture statement can be used to mark the transition between figures in a dance, stages in the development of a play, or major thought divisions in a speech. A change of picture will also support the end of a performance when it is followed by some other kind of program material. For example, it is easy to destroy the terminal impact of a song by continuing the same picture when the vocalist stops singing and begins talking to announce his next selection.

4 To punctuate, then, first perceive each of the points to be made.

5 Next ask, "Which visual elements in the scene are active in expressing this point?"—and make these the subject of your picture statement.

5.1 Sometimes there is but one element, sometimes more than one, and sometimes only part of one.

For example, you may have resolved a dramatic segment into the following statements:

(1) Here is the mother pleading with the father.

(2) Notice, their son is eavesdropping on their conversation with a rifle in his hands.

(3) Look at the father, how obdurate he remains.

(4) See the son's face tighten with grim resolve.

(5) Watch his fingers tighten on the rifle stock.

For #1, two elements are clearly necessary: mother and father.

For #2, besides the son, it is probably advisable to include the parents in order to establish that they are the subject of his eavesdropping.

Since #3 stresses the attitude of the father, he alone is important, and the other two characters are irrelevant. To include them would divide the viewer's attention and also make the father's expression smaller and less discernible, thus weakening the point.

The point of #4 is to convey the son's reaction as strongly as possible. Hence one concentrates on that portion of him where this reaction is most evident: his face.

In #5 the son's temptation to shoot is stressed by concentrating on another expressive part of him: his fingers. Although both face and fingers might have been shown simultaneously, they are more forceful when separated into two statements, following the principle of one impression at a time.

5.2 When the subject includes more than one element, ask, "What are their relative degrees of importance?"

In #1 above, for instance, if you decide that the mother and father are of equal importance, your picture composition should emphasize them equally, but it should make the mother dominant if you wish to emphasize her pleading.

5.3   Visualize how to arrange the elements to express their relationships.

In #1, perhaps you see the mother close to the father, but farther from camera than he is, to reveal more of her face than his. In #2, are the parents in the foreground with the son in the distance between them? Or is he behind a doorway in the foreground with them in the distance?

5.4   Visualize as compact an arrangement as possible in order to eliminate irrelevant material which will weaken your point.

Also avoid wasting large areas of the screen with inert material (neutral background, for example) that has nothing to communicate. In the words of a once popular song, which still deserves to be popular with directors, "Accentuate the positive, eliminate the negative."

6   After visualizing each picture statement, plan how to change from one statement to another, choosing one of the following ways:

6.1   Switch to a new shot from a different camera.

Thus, camera 1 takes a full shot of a golfer to support the point, "This is how to address the ball." Then camera 2 takes a closeup of his hands, which makes a new point, "This is the proper grip."

(Besides taking the new shot, you can, as appropriate, choose to dissolve, fade or wipe. These alternatives, which require considerable explanation, will be considered later in the book.)

6.2   Move or zoom the camera.

For example, as each member of a row of panelists is introduced, the camera pans from one to another. Or the camera opens on an interviewer and, as he mentions the interviewee, dollies back into a two-shot. Or the camera establishes an office desk, then zooms in on a ringing telephone.

6.3   Move the subject.

Even inanimate objects can sometimes be moved. For example, the camera is trained on one face of a four-sided display board; then the board is revolved to present a new face. More frequently, however, new picture statements result from human beings entering or leaving the frame or moving around within it. A seated performer may rise, making the point, "It's time to get busy!" A teacher who has been writing on a chalkboard may turn and walk forward, masking out the board, to begin some new topic such as "tomorrow's assignment." Or one of a group of actors may move from a subordinate location into what theatre people call "the upstage position," to deliver an important speech. In television, this means that he places himself farther from camera than his fellows so that, in facing them, his features are also revealed to the television viewer, whereas theirs, being turned away towards him, are more subordinated.

Movements such as these are often ignored by inexperienced directors as a way to make new picture statements. They tend to keep their performers stationary, thereby losing the animation and expression of human action and cheating the audience of its major interest in seeing people doing something.

6.4 *Have the subject move and the camera follow it.*

For instance, the camera can start with a full shot of characters A and B, then pan with B as he moves away from A and forward into a chest shot, then pull back to widen the shot as A crosses to join B. This concerted movement of camera and performers can result in any number of changing compositions, each designed to support some new point in the evolving action.

7 So far you have been advised to:

(1) Identify the points in the action.
(2) Visualize picture statements to support each point.
(3) Decide how to change from one statement to another.

In the next chapter, this procedure is applied to the planning of two complete program segments.

Chapter 2

Examples of Picture Statements

Example 1
The Guest Violinist

Participating in this program are a host and a guest violinist. It is planned that the host will have a few welcoming remarks for his viewers before introducing his guest. After chatting briefly with the guest, the host will suggest inspecting the guest's violin, which was made by a notable craftsman. Then the guest will accept the host's invitation to play a selection. This is prefaced by a short piano introduction and consists of two sections: the first *andante* (moderately slow and flowing), the second *allegro* (brisk and lively). Following this, the host will thank the guest, inform the audience about the feature on his next program, and conclude.

In some circumstances, particularly when there is a standardized setting and a routine with which the program host and the production people are familiar, the director might be expected to improvise his camerawork, punctuating the action as best he can on the spur of the moment. Here, however, it is assumed that he has an opportunity to pre-plan.

The first stage of the planning is presented below. Here are the points as the director perceives them, the pictures he visualizes to support these points, and some comments to explain his decisions:

THE POINTS	WHAT THE AUDIENCE SHOULD SEE
The host is welcoming the audience to his program.	HOST, SEEN FROM CHEST UP.

The host should be close enough to make good contact with his audience. His face is the part of him which carries the expression of welcome. A view of the guest at this moment would be irrelevant and distracting, tending to break the bond between the viewer's eyes and those of the host.

| *The host has a guest with him.* | THE PICTURE WIDENS TO REVEAL THE GUEST, SEATED CLOSE TO HOST. |

Now is the time for the guest to enter the action and, consequently, enter the picture. The host should also be seen, however, to establish his location in relation to the guest.

| *This is the kind of person the guest is.* | GUEST ALONE, SHOWN FROM CHEST UP. |

A closer, isolating shot will give the guest his due importance as the new center of interest when he first speaks. It will also give the audience a more intimate impression of him.

| *The host and guest are conversing.* | SAME TWO-SHOT AS BEFORE, WITH EMPHASIS EQUAL BETWEEN THEM. |

The shot should be compact enough to permit easy reading of their faces.

| *They are going to inspect the violin.* | BOTH, RISING AND MOVING, FRAMED MORE AND MORE CLOSELY SO THAT ON REACHING THE VIOLIN THEY ARE SEEN ONLY FROM THE WAIST UP. |

Placing the violin apart keeps it out of sight until it enters the action. This also introduces variety through movement to a new location. Narrowing framing during the move will make the violin large enough when it enters the picture to promote its prominence as the new center of interest.

This is what the violin looks like. VIOLIN (HELD BY GUEST) FRAMED CLOSE WITH BACKGROUND DEFOCUSED.

Taking the closeup and defocusing the background both serve to eliminate irrelevant material.

The host is inviting the guest to play. BOTH PERFORMERS AS BEFORE THE VIOLIN CLOSEUP.

No explanation seems necessary for this picture.

The guest prepares to play while the GUEST STEPS AWAY FROM
pianist plays the introduction. HOST AND FORWARD TO WHERE ACCOMPANIST CAN BE SEEN IN BACKGROUND.

This eliminates the host, who is no longer significant, and reveals the presence of the piano and the accompanist, keeping them subordinated, however, to the guest. The picture change also marks the beginning of the guest's musical performance, a new major section of the program.

The guest is playing an andante pas- GUEST PLAYING, VIEWED FROM
sage. ABOUT WAIST UP (PIANIST ELIMINATED)

Now all that matters is the violinist's performance. Although the truly active elements in this performance are his face, arms and violin, it would not be advisable to frame them too closely at first since closer framing will be needed to support the next passage of the music:

He is changing to an allegro passage. GUEST PLAYING, VIEWED FROM ANOTHER AND CLOSER ANGLE.

Pictorial punctuation is used to clarify a change in the pattern of the music. The closer shot should reinforce the more animated performance that results from the increased tempo; the active elements (face, arms, violin) will now make a stronger impression since they have been enlarged and given exclusive command of the frame.

He finishes the performance.   CONTINUING THE SAME SHOT,
                                              THE PICTURE WIDENS AS THE
                                              MUSIC ENDS.

The sense of completion is reinforced by a withdrawal from the performers and a progressive re-entry of the environment, creating anticipatory space for the host's re-entry. This withdrawal should also provide activity during the brief auditory pause which seems desirable here to let the spell of the music linger somewhat before the host speaks.

The host thanks the guest.   GUEST AND HOST—THE HOST
                                              SEEN FIRST IN THE REAR OF
                                              THE PICTURE, THEN MOVING
                                              UP TO THE GUEST.

Cutting from the guest alone to a two-shot of him and the host makes a more pronounced change between the musical performance and the ensuing talk than were the host to walk into the concluding shot of the performance.

The host announces the feature on his   HOST LEAVES GUEST (CAMERA
next program and concludes the show.   PANNING WITH HIM) AND
                                          MOVES CLOSER TO CAMERA
                                          TO MAKE HIS CLOSING AN-
                                          NOUNCEMENT.

Since the guest's part is over, he is eliminated from the picture. To take leave of him by panning gradually away from him seems more polite than to cut abruptly to a one-shot of the host. Having the host move nearer to the camera for his closing announcement helps to reestablish his direct contact with the viewer.

                                          CLOSING TITLES AND FADE TO
                                          BLACK.

This, of course, is not the only way to visualize the sequence. But however the director does conceive his pictures, he should have a reason, based on the points of the program, for each of them.

Planning the actual camera treatment

Now comes the last stage of the planning process: the visualized pictures must be realized in actual camera shots. To this end, the director takes pencil and paper to work out at reduced scale actual physical locations for his performers and cameras and to test, with templates of his lens angles, which lens he will use for each particular shot.[1] It is assumed here that he will be using 3″ image orthicons with lens turrets; hence the references that follow to 50mm, 135mm and 8½″ lenses. But were he to use other cameras and lenses, the principles of the planning process would still be the same.

As shown in *Figure 2/1,* the director starts with the host and guest seated in adjacent chairs, and places camera 1 for its opening shot of the host. He chooses a 50mm lens for this shot, knowing that it will permit traversing the shortest distance with the least difficulty about maintaining focus during the dolly back to include the guest. (See *Figure 2/2*) With this lens, however, he realizes that he cannot start so close to the host as to cause facial distortion through exaggerated perspective.

Having determined where camera 1 will be at the end of the dolly-back, he can now determine where the host and guest will stand after walking over to inspect the violin. He plans to have camera 1 pan them to this location. Since he does not want the violin in 1's shot of the men while they are seated, he knows that the small table on which he has decided to place the instrument must be stationed off one side of this shot. The guest's side is logical, since this will allow the guest to reach the violin without crossing in front of the host.

The shot of the men inspecting the violin should be closer than the one of them seated in order to make the image of the violin as large as possible. Therefore, the men must end their walk at a place where camera 1's lens angle is narrow enough to accomplish the closer framing. Having located this place with the help of his lens template, the director sets the table where it will guide the men into the desired position. (*Figure 2/3*)

Next, the director seeks a basic location for camera 2, which he needs for a closeup of the seated guest when he is introduced, and later for a closeup of the violin when it is being inspected. Since the guest is seated to camera left of the host, camera 2 should be on the right so that it can command an adequately full shot of the guest's face while he is looking towards the host. Also, it should be far enough from the guest in his standing position so that a long lens can be used to defocus the background in the closeup of the violin. So Camera 2 is placed as in *Figure 2/4.*

During the piano introduction to his selection, the guest can keep some visual activity going by advancing in front of the table. Meanwhile, to avoid

[1] For the process of planning shots on paper at reduced scale, see Chapter 22, "Making Floor Plans."

Fig. 2/1

Fig. 2/2

Fig. 2/3

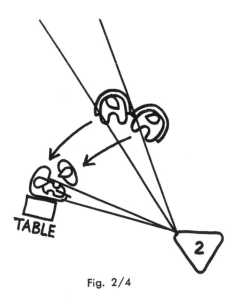

Fig. 2/4

being seen during the selection, the host can return to his chair. Camera 2 is assigned to the piano introduction, panning with the guest to his playing position, where the pianist is seen to his right in the background. By using the lens template to spot the guest and pianist within a 50mm lens angle projected from camera 2's location on the floor plan, the location of the piano can be determined, as in *Figure 2/5.*

The furniture and basic camera positions are now established. In relation to these, a drape background can also be established and the remaining shots and movements calculated.

Figure 2/6 shows locations during the violinist's perfomance. Camera 1 takes the *andante* passage. Meanwhile, camera 2 (between shots) moves in as indicated by the dash line. From this closer location it takes the *allegro* passage, at the conclusion of which (while still feeding program) it dollies back to its original location to widen the picture.

During the *allegro* passage, as shown in *Figure 2/7,* camera 1 moves left to a place from which it can show the host moving forward from his chair to thank the guest at the end of the selection. As soon as camera 1 is taken for this shot, camera 2, its mission accomplished, withdraws in order to avoid getting in the picture when the host, panned on camera 1, moves away from the guest and forward to deliver his closing remarks.

Fig. 2/5

Fig. 2/6

Fig. 2/7

The result of this plotting can be summarized as follows:

CAMERA TREATMENT	THE POINTS
1 (50mm) HOST, CHEST SHOT	HOST IS WELCOMING AUDIENCE TO PROGRAM.
DOLLY BACK TO INCLUDE GUEST	HE HAS GUEST WITH HIM.
2 (135mm) CLOSEUP GUEST	THIS IS WHAT GUEST LOOKS LIKE.
1 (50mm) BOTH (Other shots may be needed if this is a long conversation.)	HOST AND GUEST ARE CONVERSING.
PAN LEFT WITH THEM TO VIOLIN ON SMALL TABLE	THEY ARE GOING TO INSPECT VIOLIN.
2 (8½″) CLOSEUP VIOLIN	THIS IS WHAT VIOLIN LOOKS LIKE.
1 (50mm) BOTH, WAIST SHOT	HOST IS INVITING GUEST TO PLAY.
2 (50mm) PAN LEFT WITH GUEST UNTIL HE STOPS IN LEFT FOREGROUND OF SHOT WITH PIANIST IN RIGHT BACKGROUND	GUEST PREPARES TO PLAY WHILE PIANIST PLAYS INTRODUCTION. HOST, OFF CAMERA, RETURNS TO HIS CHAIR.
1 (50mm) GUEST, WAIST SHOT	GUEST IS PLAYING *ANDANTE* PASSAGE.
(2 DOLLY CLOSER FOR NEXT SHOT OF GUEST)	
2 (50mm) GUEST, CHEST SHOT	GUEST IS PLAYING *ALLEGRO* PASSAGE.
DOLLY BACK TO INCLUDE PIANIST	GUEST IS FINISHING PERFORMANCE.
(1 HAS MOVED LEFT AND BACK SOMEWHAT FOR NEXT SHOT)	
1 (50mm) BOTH, WITH HOST ADVANCING FROM RIGHT REAR	HOST MOVES UP TO THANK GUEST.
(2 WITHDRAWS)	

| PAN WITH HOST AS HE LEAVES GUEST AND APPROACHES CAMERA | HOST ANNOUNCES NEXT FEATURE AND CLOSES PROGRAM. |

With this planning accomplished, the director is ready to actually shoot the program, with reasonable assurance that the pictures which his audience sees will enhance its understanding of the structure and meaning of the program, thus accomplishing the goal of pictorial punctuation.

Example 2

Jean Learns a New Dance Step

In this sequence from a women's program, Jean, the program hostess, is to learn the fundamentals of a new dance step from a guest named Bill.

From a conference with Jean, the director learns that the dance involves the entire body, requiring full shots rather than closeups of the feet. Over opening music, Bill will dance briefly—after which Jean will ask her viewers, "Wouldn't you like to learn how this is done?" Bill will proceed to demonstrate the basic movement with Jean beside him, trying to follow his instructions. Then Jean will watch him perform two variations, trying after each to do it herself. To close, Jean will thank Bill, then invite her viewers to try the dance themselves.

As shown in *Figure 2/8,* the director decides to base his cameras about 90° apart so they can take reverse angle shots, one favoring Jean, the other Bill, at a distance sufficient to allow full length shots with their widest lenses. As playing area he chooses a corner where the studio drapes meet at right angles. With the attention on moving bodies, there is no need for elaborate scenery.

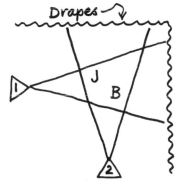

Fig. 2/8

For audio pickup the director will need either a boom or wireless chest microphones. There should be no cables trailing from the performers to impede their action and look unsightly in long shots.

Following these decisions, the director works out the sequence of picture statements below:

BILL BRIEFLY DEMONSTRATES
THE DANCE.

Bill is the dominant subject and is seen full length because his dance involves the total body. Jean is shown, too, because it's her show and because her location should be established before cutting to a one-shot of her. She has been subordinated, however, by being placed in the distance. Perched on a stool, she contrasts with Bill's standing figure. To motivate a cut to her, she applauds Bill's performance, and he turns towards her in acknowledgment.

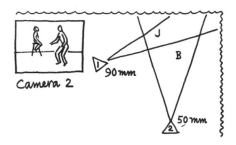

JEAN ORIENTS THE AUDIENCE.

"That was the (name of dance). Like to learn it? Let's ask Bill to show us how." The shot should be close enough to give Jean eye contact with her viewers, but not too abrupt a change in scale from the preceding long shot. The selection of a lens depends not only on the initial framing of Jean by herself, but also on the framing of her with Bill after the camera has panned with her to him.

BILL WILL GLADLY TEACH HER.

This framing should favor Bill and be close enough to show his face clearly. After a few sentences, Bill invites Jean to stand beside him. Her move to do so cues the next shot.

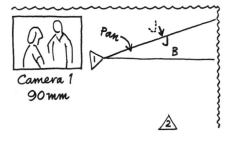

JEAN LEARNS THE
FUNDAMENTALS.

This is a full shot of both performers, equidistant from camera
since interest should be distributed
equally between them.

BILL DEMONSTRATES
VARIATION #1.

Attention should center now on
Bill. Hence, have him move away
from Jean and face her, taking him
with the camera which favors him.
A full view is still needed of him, but
not of her.

JEAN TRIES THE VARIATION.

Take the other camera as interest now passes to her.

BILL DEMONSTRATES
VARIATION #2

and

JEAN TRIES IT.

These shots are the same as for
the first variation.

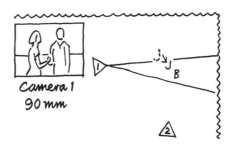

JEAN MOVES IN TO THANK BILL,
WHO IN TURN CONGRATULATES
HER.

Pan with Jean into a two-shot
favoring Bill and close enough to
show his expression clearly. He deserves the major emphasis as the
guest who is being thanked for his
performance.

JEAN REACTS TO HIS
COMPLIMENT.

A matching two-shot from the other camera favors Jean.

JEAN ADDRESSES THE
AUDIENCE.

Camera 2
90 mm

"If *I* can do it, *you* can, so why not try it?" To mark her shift of attention from Bill to the audience, have her walk closer to camera. This will give her dominance over Bill, who remains in the background.

END OF SEQUENCE

Aided by the two examples you have just read and by the chapter which preceded them, you should be able to start planning television picture statements which will interpret accurately the structure and meaning of your program to its audience.

While you are planning, remember:

From moment to moment throughout the program there are different points to be conveyed.

Different points involve different visual subjects.

To make each point definitely, frame prominently the relevant subject, or part thereof, or group of subjects.

When more than one subject is included in the frame, reveal and emphasize these subjects in proportion to their relative importance in making the point at hand.

The resultant arrangement is your picture statement.

When a new point is to be made, change to a new picture statement.

Chapter 3

A Moment-by-Moment Questionnaire

At every moment the picture you show should make the point to be made at that moment. To assess how well it will do so, it is helpful to ask a number of critical questions. Three of these should already be evident from your reading of the preceding chapters:

Am I conscious of the point?
What visual subjects convey it?
Are they included in my picture?

But there are six more useful questions to be asked:

Can the subjects be seen clearly?
Do they preserve their natural and characteristic form?
Does your picture make a single, dominant impression?
Is it free of distractions and discomforts?
Is it sufficiently animated?
Does it make the point expressively?

You should ask these questions throughout the whole production process, during your planning as well as while you are watching the control room monitors. They are useful for evaluating every factor of your pictorial composition: the relation of your subject to its background and to the camera, the effect of the video control adjustments, the choice of a lens and of its aperture, the design of the setting, the action of the performers, and even the selection of their wearing apparel.

Each of the next six chapters will be devoted to one of the questions and to the production conditions which must be achieved in order to answer the question affirmatively. Although some of these conditions may be familiar to you under such categories as lighting, staging, performing, and camera operation, you will find them classified here rather differently—not by crafts, but by communication purposes which the crafts should serve. This may help you to evaluate the crafts in a new and useful light.

It should also help to accustom you to a director's way of looking, for a director is concerned not with one craft at a time, but with the interrelationship of all of them. When deciding where a performer will stand, for instance, he may take into account the need for backlight, the color and pattern of the background, the elevation of the camera, and what visual elements will be in focus on a particular lens at a certain distance and with a given intensity of illumination. When viewing a picture or planning one, he evaluates more or less simultaneously all of the various factors which combine to make up its appearance.

In conducting such an evaluation, you will find it useful to apply the Moment-by-Moment Questionnaire.

Chapter 4

Visual Clarity

Whatever has meaning to communicate must be clearly perceived by the audience. Evident as this requirement may seem, it cannot be achieved without conscious effort. Cameras must be aimed from revealing angles. Subjects must be related to the proper cameras. They must be kept in frame and focus. They must be framed closely enough to reveal their significant details. Their form must be brought out by proper brightness levels and not obscured by other elements of the picture.

As a director, you are responsible for seeing that these conditions are achieved. Therefore:

1 Aim your cameras from revealing angles.

Relate the positions of camera and subject so as to reveal the most communicative aspect of the subject. Nine times out of ten with human subjects, it is important to reveal facial expressions.

1.1 When performers are interacting with each other, cross your cameras.

Don't shoot as in *Figure 4/1* using the camera on the right to take the person on the right and the camera on the left to take the person on the left,

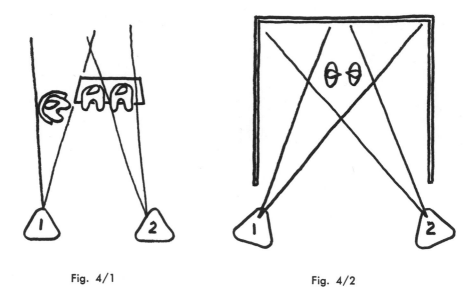

Fig. 4/1   Fig. 4/2

for when the performers are looking towards each other, these shots will take only profiles—and one eye, one eyebrow, one nostril, and only half a mouth are liable to reveal only half of what a face is communicating. Therefore, cross your cameras: right camera on left performer, left camera on right performer.

1.2   Remember the need to show faces when devising your floor plan.

The setting in *Figure 4/2* is so narrow and deep that the cameras cannot spread far enough apart to take much more than profiles. More advantageous camera angles are provided by a wedge- or L-shaped setting. Occasionally, directors also design openings in the walls through which cameras can shoot without being noticed, or employ "wild walls" which can be moved aside for certain shots.

How do you cover the conference set-up in *Figure 4/3* if you are allowed only two cameras? With this arrangement it is impossible to reveal clearly the faces of all participants. As the cameras are stationed in the diagram, each covers one side of the table adequately, but neither will show the face of the person at the end of the table.

In the kitchen set in *Figure 4/4,* there are no stations from which cameras can reveal more than profiles of the performers when they are using the counters, sink, stove and refrigerator.

Fig. 4/3

Fig. 4/4

Fig. 4/5

Fig. 4/6

1.3   Work for the most revealing camera angles when planning your shot alterations.

Figure 4/5 shows how a student director planned a demonstration of potato printing.

Camera 2 took the opening title on an easel. Next, camera 1 established the teacher at the table, dollied in to a chest shot of her, then tilted down to her hands working with materials on the table surface. This shot of the hands was alternated with wider shots of the teacher taken by camera 2. Just before the end of the sequence at the table, camera 1 (between shots) pulled back to its starting position. From there it panned with the teacher to the display board and remained on her there as she showed examples of finished prints, which were taken in closeup by camera 2.

This treatment was deficient in clarity. The wide lens which camera 1 needed on its first shot to establish the teacher at the table proved too wide, when the camera tilted down, for closeups of her hands. Also, as shown in *Figure 4/6,* camera 1's pan with the teacher to the display board ended in too loose a shot, which moreover showed the teacher back-to, with the

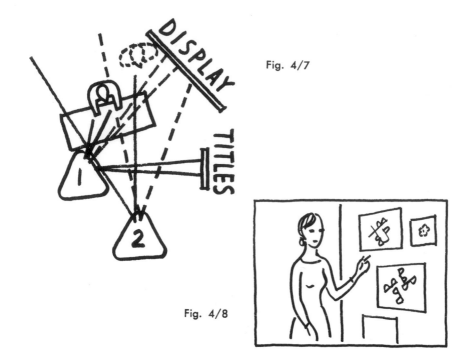

Fig. 4/7

Fig. 4/8

display board sloping so much into the distance that the display seemed to be presented to some offstage observer rather than to the television viewer.

An improved treatment is diagrammed in *Figure 4/7.* Here, camera 2 takes all the wide shots of the teacher, both at the table and at the display board. As can be seen by comparing *Figures 4/6* and *4/8,* the revised framing of the display board is clearer, not only because the teacher is closer, but also because she is turned towards the audience. Camera 1 takes all closeups, of both the displayed prints and the table demonstration, getting a closer, hence clearer view of the latter because its lens can be selected solely for that purpose.

The improved version could have been devised on paper before bringing the program into the studio, where time is too precious to waste on needless revisions.

2   Relate the action to the proper camera.

The best planned camera treatment can be defeated by a performer who plays to the wrong camera.

2.1   Be sure that performers understand their relation to the cameras.

Although it's inadvisable to burden a performer with unnecessary information, acquaint him with what he needs to know about the cameras—which one will take the closeup of the property he's holding, which one he should address when the film insert ends, and so on.

If he's new to television, he'll need to realize that the camera with the red light shining is the one that's "on."

If you change his action during rehearsal, have him show you that he understands the change by actually performing it. Even with experienced talent, it is rarely safe to assume that your instructions will be interpreted accurately.

2.2   Keep your camera plan as simple and consistent as possible.

In the revised version of the potato printing demonstration, one camera was used consistently for views of the teacher and the other for close-ups of her material. Thus, there was little chance that she would present either her face or her material to the wrong camera.

3   Prevent masking the subject from camera.

3.1   Performers' hands should not mask essential information.

Obviously, the audience will not be able to read the label on a bottle if it is covered by the hand holding the bottle.

It is frustrating when hands which are writing on chalkboards or other vertical surfaces cover the letters as they are being formed. A long-handled chalk holder or felt pen will keep the hand below the line of writing—or the performer can be taught, as in *Figure 4/9,* to work from the camera right side of the board (assuming that he is right-handed). This also opens his face and body to the camera, which in turn helps to pick up his voice on a boom microphone, since there will be no room to get

Fig. 4/9

the microphone in front of him if he is facing close in to the vertical surface.

3.2   Keep performers from covering other performers who ought to be seen.

Even when they have rehearsed their positions, inexperienced performers may fail to duplicate these positions in performance. It may help, during rehearsal, to have them sight coordinates by which they can orient themselves. ("I'm in front of the right end of the sofa and just opposite the window in the left wall.") Sometimes you can direct them in relation to the furniture. ("Stand beside the arm chair, then cross to behind the desk.") Critical locations can be marked on the floor with chalk, water paint or masking tape.

Even when they hit their marks, they may be covered or be covering someone else because the camera is off its position. Hence, critical camera positions may also need to be marked.

4 Keep the subject in frame.

4.1 When framing, keep important elements away from the edges of the picture.

Although visible on control room monitors, these elements may not appear on less carefully adjusted home receivers.

Lettering on cards which are to be taken by studio cameras should be indented at least $\frac{1}{6}$th of the height and width of the framed area, as shown in *Figure 4/10*. Outside this area there should be a margin to keep the camera from accidentally shooting off the edge of the card.

Fig. 4/10

4.2 Work with performers on keeping in frame.

Caution inexperienced performers against making abrupt and unevenly paced movements unless these have been successfully rehearsed on camera. Otherwise, they may walk out of frame before the camera can pan with them, or rise and decapitate themselves, so to speak, before the camera can tilt up.

In ad-libbed situations they can signal their intentions of moving. They can do this either verbally ("Now, over on the workbench we have . . .") or visually, as when placing their hands on the arms of their chair and shifting their weight before rising.

Performers who are handling small objects should be taught not to gesticulate broadly with them or pick them up suddenly. It may be advisable for beginners to keep the objects in constant contact with a table surface to inhibit their being waved around at random.

4.3   Framing also depends on the camerawork.

Rapidly moving subjects are difficult to keep framed properly when they are followed in too tight a shot. Frame them rather loosely if your cameraman is not expert.

When panning laterally moving subjects, it is customary to "lead" them, allowing more space ahead than behind them. While partly for compositional balance as will be explained later, this also helps to prevent the subject from nosing out of the frame during unexpected spurts.

When two or more performers move at once, as do the host and guest approaching the violin in Chapter 2, they may separate beyond the limits of the frame. Instead of trying to contain them both, it is preferable to frame the leader acceptably and let the follower re-enter the frame at destination.

5   Keep the subject in focus.

Although you sometimes want the background out of focus to stand your subjects out against it, almost invariably you want the subjects themselves sharp and clear. Their being so depends on the depth of field, i.e. the distance between the nearest and farthest subject which will appear acceptably focused at a given lens setting. The greater the depth of field, the less focusing problem you will have when:

. . . subjects are at different distances from the lens.

. . . the subject is very close to the lens.

. . . the camera must pan from a near subject to a more distant one, or vice versa.

. . . the distance between camera and subject is altered either by the camera or the subject moving forward or back.

Here are some suggestions to apply to such conditions:

5.1   Consider the illumination.

Adding more light to the scene will permit the lens to be stopped down. The smaller the diaphragm opening, the greater the depth of field.

5.2   Consider your choice of a lens.

You can attain greater depth of field by changing to a lens of shorter focal length—but only if you accept the consequently wider framing. If you move the camera closer to approximate the framing as it was before the lens change, the depth of field will be reduced again.

It does pay, however, to use a short focal length lens when either the subject or the camera is moving in or out. In fact, don't expect an inexperienced cameraman to maintain focus while dollying on anything longer than his standard short focal length lens.

When you want to go from wide to close more swiftly than a cameraman can maintain focus, consider using a varifocal (zoom) lens. This will keep focused throughout the zoom when pre-set for the distance which exists between the camera and the subject. If either subject or camera moves appreciably to change this distance, however, the lens will have to be refocused. Furthermore, you should consider whether the zoom will harmonize in appearance with the dolly movements you may have used elsewhere in the program. On a dolly-in (as when one walks in), closer subjects enlarge more than distant ones, whereas on a zoom-in their relative sizes remain unaltered.

When a subject can be brought no closer to the lens without going out of focus, try a lens of shorter focal length. The shorter the focal length, the closer the subject can be focused. There is a catch to this, however: unless the subject is flat and perpendicular to the camera's axis of vision, it will appear increasingly distorted, the closer it comes to the lens.

5.3   Consider the distance setting of the lens.

When your subject is too close to the lens to be focused with the normal control for following focus, try adjusting the distance setting on the lens barrel, moving it from infinity, where it is likely to be set, to the actual distance in feet that exists between the subject and the lens.

5.4   Consider the camera angle.

Occasionally, as when shooting a chessboard, you may have difficulty getting equal focus on small objects (such as the chessmen) which lie at different distances from the lens. By shooting at a steeper downward angle, you can diminish the span between the nearest and farthest subject over which the focus has to be distributed.

5.5   Help inexperienced cameramen to improve their focusing ability.

When depth of field is shallow and you need equal focus on two sub-jects at unequal distances from camera, your cameraman may need to learn that, to split his focus, he should focus—not halfway between the subjects —but at roughly one third of the distance from the nearest to the farthest.

To let him give utmost attention to following focus during a straight dolly movement, you can sometimes suggest that he lock unneeded mobile parts such as the pedestal elevating device, horizontal pan head, or tripod wheels. If jurisdictional rules permit, you can also enlist someone to move the camera mount, thus freeing the cameraman to use one hand for focusing and the other (if need be) for panning or tilting.

When he has to pan between a close and distant subject, you may need to allow him some practice time. During this, if he will note and remember how much he has to turn his focusing control, he should be able to change focus while he is panning without waiting for the new subject to come into view.

6   Frame closely enough to reveal the important details.

Loosely framed subjects can be indistinct because they are too small on the screen and spread over too few scanning lines to be resolved with suffi-cient definition. Hence:

6.1   Generally restrict wide shots to:

. . . framing broad physical movement, as in dance or sports, where interest is on movement rather than facial expressions.

. . . establishing an overall situation by showing the presence and relative locations of its participants.

. . . showing the total environment in which the action occurs.

6.2   Otherwise, rely mainly on medium shots and closeups, framing only what is meaningful at the moment.

Constantly ask whether you are shooting close enough. Is reference being made to the whole violin or merely to its bridge? How close does the master of ceremonies have to be before you feel that he is really talking to you?

6.3   For shooting close, will you move the camera in, or use a long focal length lens?

Using the long lens allows you to keep the camera at a distance which will permit all lenses on its turret to be used for subsequent shots. A camera which is too close to its subject may lack time to move out for its next, wider shot. It may also interfere with another camera's shot, or disturb the performers' concentration, or introduce blower noise into the microphone.

The camera must come close, however, if you want a down-angled closeup (as when showing the contents of a bowl) and cannot elevate the camera on a crane to get this angle from a greater distance, or wish to avoid using a mirror to reflect an overhead view.

6.4 When a camera mount is stopped from coming close enough, as by the front side of a desk or counter:

. . . see whether the distance between camera and subject can be lessened by revolving the base of the tripod or pedestal to present a flat side to the furniture, or

. . . consider substituting furniture with an opening into which the base of the camera mount can penetrate.

6.5 When closeups are to be taken, make the subjects conveniently large if you can control their size.

The smaller the subject, the more difficult it is to frame closely. Musical notation, snapshot photographs, diagrams occupying partial pages of books, and the like will benefit from enlargement if they are to be taken by a studio camera. As appropriate, you can have them re-drawn, or get photographic blowups made of them, or convert them to slides for rear-screen projection.

6.6 Closeups of miniature subjects are more easily shot in limbo.

When closeups are needed of miniature subjects (coins, stamps, watch dials, etc.) which are being used by the performers, you can try to get duplicates of them to be shot in limbo (i.e. in some convenient place outside the playing area) by a camera which has sufficient opportunity to frame and focus them properly from as close a distance as necessary.

Shooting in limbo will give the cameraman a better opportunity to focus more closely, if need be, by changing the distance setting on his lens barrel. It will also allow him to move close enough to the subject to use an extreme wide angle lens. As previously explained, this can take bigger closeups than any longer lens because it can come extremely close to the subject and still stay in focus. Since depth of field in this case is particularly shallow, however, the subject must be such that all visible parts of it are approximately equidistant from the lens. Furthermore, special care must be taken to prevent a shadow of the camera from obscuring the subject.

6.7   Closeups of small, static subjects can be photographed in advance and used as slides, projected in telecine.

This avoids having to divert a studio camera from the main action for the length of time it may take to frame and focus the subject properly.

6.8   Proportion your subject, when possible, to a 3 × 4 ratio.

Although sufficiently large in actuality, some subjects may not appear large enough on the screen because their proportions do not suit the 3 × 4 aspect ratio of the screen. When they are tall and narrow or low and broad, and must be shown in entirety, the camera may have to move back so far to encompass them that their details will be illegible. Therefore, any graphic material which is to be framed as a whole in closeup should be prepared in a 3 × 4 ratio. The teacher who is putting a long sentence on the chalkboard should be asked to write it in several short lines rather than a single extended one. And the chorus in two rows of twelve persons should be regrouped into four rows of six persons, if it can still sing well in this new arrangement.

6.9   Restrict the number of elements per line.

The more elements which must appear side by side in the picture, the wider the framing must be, hence the smaller and less distinct the elements will appear. Therefore, one should restrict the number of characters per line in printed titles and captions. For the same reason, groups of singers or dancers which were originally constituted to fill the breadth of a theatre stage may need, for television, to be reduced in membership and reorganized more compactly.

6.10   Bring performers as close together as possible.

The nearer performers play to each other, the more closely the camera can frame them. It is surprising how close they can be to each other without appearing unnatural on the screen.

6.11   Shoot wide subjects from a side angle.

When persons need to be separated by the requirements of the action
yet still need to be included in the same frame, the screen distance between
them can be reduced by shooting them from the side, as camera 2 is doing
in *Figure 4/11*. Notice how much
more discernible the features will be
in 2's shots than in 1's. Similarly, an
angled shot can be used to enlarge
the screen size of the members of
large groups such as vocal choruses.

The side angle is useful not
only with stationary groupings, but
also for movements which carry persons away from each other. If taken
from the front, dancers who separate
widely can cause problems: the camera may not be able to dolly back as
quickly as they separate; yet if it pans
with only one of them, the choreo-
graphic relationship between them
will be lost. An angle shot, however,
will contain the entire movement.

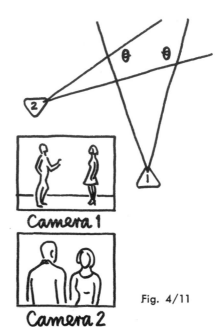

Camera 1

Camera 2

Fig. 4/11

6.12   Deploy your subjects in depth.

The movement of the dancers in the angle shot just cited will tend to be
more parallel than perpendicular to the camera's line of vision. This illustrates a difference between blocking action for television and for the stage.
Since a theatre stage extends across the spectators' line of vision, the axis
for movement and placement of characters on it tends to run from side to
side. The television "stage," however, is the angle embraced by the camera
lens, a truncated pyramid of space widening away from the lens, which
invites the placement and movement of subjects in depth. Such deployment,
as already demonstrated, helps to reduce needless screen distance between
the subjects.

6.13   Place small subjects closer to the lens, big ones farther from it.

Within the camera's expanding angle, a small subject close to the lens can fill the entire screen. As distance from the lens increases, it takes more subjects or larger subjects to fill the screen. Applications of this fact are illustrated in *Figures 4/12* and *4/13*. In *Figure 4/12* the telephone, as principal subject, has been placed in the foreground, where its screen size exceeds that of the two persons behind it. In *Figure 4/13* three subjects of different size have been arranged so that they can be panned by a single camera and command equal size on the screen. This principle of arrangement should be kept in mind when blocking a one-camera program or any sequence where a second camera is not available to permit lens changes for framing subjects of different sizes.

Fig. 4/12

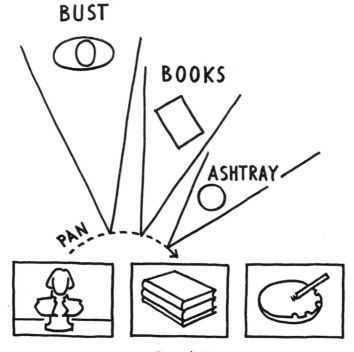

Fig. 4/13

7 Bring out clarity of form by proper brightness levels.

The form of subjects on the television screen is rendered by phosphorescent particles glowing at various degrees of brightness. In order for these brightness differences to clearly define the subjects, production people—under the ultimate supervision of the director—must present to the camera visual material which the electronic system is capable of reproducing faithfully. One of the requirements for satisfactory reproduction is proper lighting.

7.1   See that there is sufficient light on the subject.

Too little light will obscure the picture with vibrating specks called "snow or "noise," and in color television will damage color fidelity. At present, indeed, color can require up to four times as much illumination as monochrome since the light which enters the color camera is divided between several pickup tubes and part of it is lost at the mirrors and filters on the paths to these tubes.

Directors sometimes cause problems of insufficient illumination by prescribing an effect which the system cannot reproduce. For example, if you want dark tones to simulate night or to create a somber mood, do not expect all of the light sources to be reduced uniformly. Although the instruments providing general illumination can be dimmed, some of the highlight sources should be left undimmed. The highlights are needed both to satisfy engineering requirements and because, without them for contrast, the other areas of the screen will not appear sufficiently dark.

7.2   Particularly in monochrome television, provide enough brightness difference to establish the form of your subjects.

In color television forms can be partly distinguished by contrasts of hue, but in monochrome you must rely altogether on brightness differences. When these are not taken into account, two contrasting hues may reproduce as similar shades of gray, showing little difference between a dancer's complexion and her leotard, or between faces and their background.

Brightness differences depend not only on the tonal gradations inherent in the subjects, but also on how the subjects are lighted. If faces and background are the same shade of gray under equal illumination, they can be distinguished from each other by putting more illumination on the performers and less on the background. To do this, however, you must keep the background far enough behind the performers so that the light used on them will not spill onto it.

7.3   Do not exceed the contrast range of which the system is capable.

There is a limit to the range of brightness which the system can reproduce, just as with any other medium of reproduction. In a pencil drawing,
for instance, the darkest tone achievable is governed by the blackness of
the lead, and the lightest by the tone of the paper. Television likewise has
restrictions; it cannot reproduce extremely dark and extremely bright elements with the same lens setting. If the lens is opened to expose gradations
in the darkest tones, very light gradations such as those in the performers'
faces are liable to be washed out. Or when the lens is stopped down to expose the faces properly, gradations in the darker tones are liable to appear
uniformly black on the screen.

Therefore, avoid including extremely light and dark elements in the
same scene. Expect to cause the video engineer and lighting men some
trouble if you let your performers wear starchy white shirts with very dark
suits. If you intend to stage a scene cameo-style in pools of light against
blackness, be sure that enough time is allotted for adjusting the illumination
and the camera control settings.

*7.4   Be careful about panning or zooming between very bright and
very dark subjects.*

Unless the lens opening can be adjusted remotely or automatically,
don't expect to pan with a person as he moves from a dim interior into
bright sunlight, or to zoom in from a predominantly light poster to a predominantly dark photograph included in it.

*7.5   When there is a wide inherent brightness contrast in the subject,
hold down the lighting contrast.*

Suppose, for example, that under even illumination the lightest area of
the subject is ten times brighter than the darkest—a ratio of 10:1. Then
you apply four times as much light to one side of the subject as to the
other—a ratio of 4:1. Multiplying these ratios gives a total contrast ratio of
40:1, meaning that the lightest area is now forty times brighter than the
darkest. At this writing, 40:1 is the limit recommended for monochrome
television. For color it is 20:1, which requires fairly flat and even lighting
for the average subject.

7.6   Avoid extreme changes of illumination.

These result not only from turning lights on and off and dimming them
up and down, but also if you:

. . . have a performer walk towards the source of a horizontal light beam, thus becoming subject to the "inverse square law": having covered half the distance to the source, he becomes not twice but approximately four times as bright.

. . . call for the follow-spot which has been lighting the vocal quartet to be focused down on the soloist who comes next, thus taking light which has been spread over four persons and concentrating it all on one.

7.7 *Supply film and slides which do not vary inconsistently in density.*

What has been said about extreme brightness differences in the scene applies also to changes in the density of projected materials. Film shots which vary from differences in exposure can be evened out at the laboratory during printing. When slides vary, the video engineer can make shading adjustments if he has time to see and work on them before they are switched into the program. If they are all on the same camera chain, however, and taken in direct succession, he cannot see them before they are switched; hence his shading adjustments will be seen by the audience. Loading the slides alternately on two camera chains will prevent this difficulty, provided that the director does not take them in such quick succession that the shading cannot be accomplished between takes.

It is true that some telecine cameras are equipped with automatic brightness compensators. These are corrective devices, however, and do not alter the desirability of having film and slides properly exposed in the first place.

7.8 *Cooperate with the lighting crew.*

Give them advance information about the positions of your performers, scenic elements, cameras, and overhead microphones. Give them ample time to set their instruments and illumination levels. It will not help if you dry rehearse during lighting set-up, occupying places where they need to walk or place ladders.

7.9 *Cooperate with the video engineer.*

Be willing to listen to his recommendations. If there is but one intercommunication system, avoid using it during his time to talk through it about camera alignment. Avoid retaining the cameras just before air or taping time when they are needed for rebalancing. When rehearsal time is limited, spare some of it to show the video engineer any parts of your program which contain sudden or wide variations in brightness; and if there is no rehearsal, at least forewarn him about these parts so that he can be ready to try to compensate for them by his shading adjustments. In obliging him, you are obliging yourself; it's the clarity of your program that's at stake.

8   Don't mix up the image of a principal subject with other pictorial elements.

8.1   Avoid scrambled superimposures.

Don't super the guest's name right across his face. Don't allow ghosted hands on a keyboard to claw at the pianist's face.

When setting up a super, have the detail in the frame of one camera coincide with plain area in the frame of the other camera. Be sure that each cameraman knows the precise composition of his shot, making guide marks for it, if necessary, on his viewfinder. If your system permits, preview the super before using it.

8.2   Don't let the contour of your subject blend into a visual element which it is overlapping.

Don't let the boiled egg get lost in the slice of bread behind it, or the face of the girl on the sofa get confused with the peonies in the bowl on the table behind her.

9   Avoid visuals which are rendered in needlessly fine detail.

The 525-line system used for broadcasting in the United States is not particularly noted for its ability to resolve fine detail, nor do television viewers ordinarily have much time to scrutinize a complicated image before it disappears from the screen. For sufficient clarity, therefore, make your visuals as bold and simple as possible. For example, since the thin lines of many standard maps are less than satisfactory on camera, it is advisable to have the maps redrawn, simplifying their complexity and rendering them in bolder lines and masses.

Chapter 5

Preserving Form

Do the subjects as pictured on the screen look natural and acceptable to the viewer? Despite their artificiality, he should be able to recognize what they represent, find them looking as he expects them to look, and believe in them. To help him do so, follow these recommendations:

1 Choose your camera angles with regard for the normal and natural appearance of the subject.

1.1 Shoot from the angle which promotes most ready recognition.

Neither a shoe nor a shoe brush can be readily recognized from an end view at lens level. A potter's wheel and a plate of hors d'oeuvres are more easily identified from a downward than a horizontal line of view. And a box, to read as a box, should present three planes to the camera (top and two sides) instead of only two planes or one.

1.2 Normally avoid upward or downward angles towards the human face.

It is usually advisable to show things as your viewer is accustomed to picture them. Unless you aim for intentional distortion, avoid inclined angles up or down when shooting the human face. A camera on a tripod is usually fixed at a height above the faces of seated persons and below those of standing ones. Hence, the closer it comes, the more it will have to tilt either up or down, showing either too much chin or too much pate and, if the lens has a short focal length, foreshortening the subjects' heads unnaturally. By pulling the camera back and using a longer lens, you can minimize the angle of tilt and show the faces from a more favorable level.

1.3   Avoid angled closeups of rectangular subjects such as title cards or pictures mounted on vertical surfaces.

The viewer expects to see these looking four-square, not "keystoned," i.e. with two opposite sides tapering as on the keystone of an arch. To avoid keystoning them, be sure that your cameras aim perpendicularly at their centers. When they are mounted in a row to be viewed one after another, do not pan them unless the camera is sufficiently far back to make its angle towards either end of the row almost unnoticeable. Instead, if the row is vertical, pedestal or boom up or down; or if horizontal, truck from one subject to another.

When the subjects are to be taken in limbo, it is sometimes easier, rather than moving the camera past them, to move them past the camera by mounting them on a sliding strip or title rolling device. To pan them without keystoning, you can mount them on the curving surface of a "pan board," which is concentric with the arc traveled by the panning lens.

2   Avoid distortion from extreme-angle lenses.

An extreme wide-angle lens, used too close, will make the nearer portions of the subject look abnormally larger than the more distant portions, resulting in huge noses or in enormous hands and feet when these are extended towards the lens. Unless you intend such distortion, pull the camera back and use a narrower lens.

Quite an opposite effect is produced by a telephoto or extreme narrow-angle lens. When this is used for a close shot from a great distance, spatial depth seems to be flattened out, lacking the diminishing effect of normal perspective. Thus, a shot from a theatre balcony can make the keyboard of a piano onstage look compressed and rectangular, or a shot from the bleachers behind home plate at a baseball game can make the pitcher look as large as the batter.

Time as well as space seems to be altered with extreme-angle lenses. Because the pitcher seems close to the batter on a telephoto shot, he will seem to take abnormally long to walk between his mound and home plate.

With the wide-angle lens, on the other hand, forward and backward movements seem unusually rapid, with the moving subjects swiftly enlarging or diminishing. Hence this lens can be used intentionally to add force to a boxer's punch, speed to an oncoming train, or shock when an assailant attacks the hero from behind.

3   Create an illusion of three-dimensional form.

Since television is viewed on a two-dimensional surface, an illusion of space and form must be created by artificial means. Some of these means are as follows:

3.1   *Shoot the action from a variety of angles.*

Take the opportunity offered by multiple and mobile cameras to shoot the action from various sides. Action in television does not have to be viewed from only one direction as in the theatre. Your cameras can get right on stage, as it were, and move around the scene, shooting from enough directions to make the environment really seem to surround the action instead of backing it up from one side.

3.2   *Move your performers.*

You can create more awareness of space by moving your performers through space than by keeping them stationary. Unlike actors on a proscenium stage, who have to favor the auditorium, television performers can face and move naturally in many directions. Don't be reluctant to show their backs occasionally; you can get them face-on from another camera when you need to.

3.3   *Use moving camera shots.*

Dollying in past performers and scenic objects gives a sense of penetrating space. Camera motion also makes one aware of space by creating shifting planes. When the camera dollies in, foreground elements enlarge and rise more than background elements. When the camera trucks across a scene, the foreground elements pass by more quickly than the background elements, an effect which you have probably also observed from a moving car or train.

3.4   *Show receding planes.*

It is common for beginning directors to line up a desk or counter parallel to the background and shoot it from front and center. This makes the background surface and the frontal plane of the furniture extend in height and breadth but not in depth, so that the composition is largely two-dimensional.

For a more vigorous sense of three dimensions, show receding planes. Take angle shots of walls and furniture to make them slant back in space and show their intersecting planes. Instead of lining up performers across the camera's line of vision, let them turn their bodies at angles to the camera and group in receding lines and triangles. Don't hesitate, when occasion offers, to let them overlap one another; this permits closer shots and stimulates depth perception by emphasizing that one is in front of the other. In wide shots it is often effective to stress the receding plane of the floor as the base on which your spatial composition is deployed. This can be done by using rugs on it, throwing shadows on it, and by patterning it with paint or masking tape.

3.5 Emphasize volume and space in your settings.

Settings look more three-dimensional when they contain receding elements, openings through which vistas can be seen, recesses to create pockets of space, and volumes projecting out into space or totally surrounded by it. Objects in the foreground, besides helping to create an illusion that the action is enclosed on four sides, also provide a frontal frame of reference against which to measure the recession in depth of other scenic elements.

3.6 Make foreground elements stand out against their background.

On the two-dimensional screen, things which are actually at different distances may seem to be in the same plane unless artificial means are used to reinforce their separation. One means is to focus more sharply on the near subjects than the far ones. Thus, performers can be stood out against their background, provided that the background is far enough behind them to lie beyond the limit of the depth of field.

With ample distance between performers and background it also becomes possible to stand the performers out by means of lighting. As previously explained, light can be concentrated on the playing area without spilling onto the background, allowing the latter to be lighted independently to whatever degree seems desirable. Furthermore, use can be made of backlight—light slanted down towards the performers from the side opposite camera, to rim their heads and shoulders with a bright outline. If the background is too close, this light will fall too steeply, becoming toplight rather than backlight and producing unattractive shadows.

For standing out subjects in color television, use can be made of advancing and receding hues. The "warm" hues (reds, oranges, and yellows) seem to advance closer to the beholder than the "cool" ones (blues and greens). This is true at least if other dimensions of the colors are equal.

A color can vary in three dimensions. "Hue" distinguishes it as red, green, blue, or whatever. "Saturation" distinguishes between a vivid color and a duller, grayed-down, "desaturated" one. "Brightness" refers to whether the color is light (a tint) or dark (a shade); this is the only dimension in which color is rendered in monochorome television.

Assuming their saturation and brightness to be the same, then, a warm hue will seem to advance more than a cool one. Otherwise, a lighter or a more saturated color may seem to advance more than a darker or less saturated one.

Whatever the case, you should keep the color of the background from seeming to be closer to the viewer than the persons who are playing in front of it.

3.7 Bring out form with modeling light.

The form of three-dimensional subjects can be enhanced by modeling light—light coming sufficiently from one side of camera to produce on the subject visible highlights and shadows. The contrast between highlight and shadow should be restrained unless some dramatic effect is intended, and even then should be kept within the tolerable contrast range. In color television, at the time of writing, the contrast must be less than in monochrome. This causes little hardship, however, for whereas, in monochrome, brightness differences are the sole means of conveying pictorial information, color has two other dimensions which can be varied and consequently needs less reliance on brightness differences.

3.8 Use spotlights rather than sources of flat illumination.

If modeling light is minimized, the front light (that aimed from the direction of the camera) should be such as to produce advancing highlights on the bridge of the nose and the high spots of forehead, cheekbones, and chin. Such highlights are produced by spotlight beams rather than by the diffuse illumination emitted from scoops.

For all ways to enhance form and space by lighting, spotlights, indeed, are the instruments to use. Because their light can be concentrated into beams, they produce sharper rim lighting when used as backlights. Because the beams can be aimed in specific directions, they can be kept from spilling undesired light on backgrounds and, when used for modeling, they will produce more discernible shadows. Instruments without lenses, such as the scoops, are needed for lightening excessive shadows and evening out unwanted irregularities in the lighting distribution, but if used exclusively, will flatten out space and form rather than enhance them.

4   In color television, promote conditions for achieving color fidelity.

Except for stylized effects, the colors in color television must appear as natural as possible—particularly those of human flesh and of commercial products, for which the audience has ready standards of comparison. To help insure color fidelity in his productions, it is desirable for the director to understand factors which affect the appearance of color in television.

4.1   The color of the subject is affected by the color of the illumination.

Color is a sensation produced in the brain, normally as a result of light striking the retina of the eye. According to a prevalent and useful theory, light travels in waves of different lengths, each length producing a different hue sensation and ranging from 400 millimicrons for blue to somewhat over 700 for red. White light is a mixture of all wavelengths within this range.

Wavelengths figure in the theory of selective absorption, which provides a physical explanation for the appearance of colored material. Under white light, the material will absorb certain wavelengths from that light and reflect others which, reaching an observer, will stimulate his sensation of a particular hue. Thus, "red" material is so structured that it absorbs all but the wavelengths around 700 millimicrons, which are the "red" wavelengths.

For the material to appear red, however, the light must contain red wavelengths to be reflected. It will look red under red light and under white light (which has red wavelengths in it), but under pure green or blue light it will look black.

A "black" material absorbs all wavelengths, therefore reflecting none. A "white" material reflects all the wavelengths it receives, looking white under white light, red under red light, and so on.

This is the theory. In practice, colored light is rarely restricted to a single wavelength, and materials rarely reflect only one wavelength or a narrowly confined band of wavelengths; hence the results are not so easily predictable. Caucasian flesh under green light, for example, will go dark but not black and, reflecting some green, will take on a quite unwholesome appearance.

The essential thing to remember is that the color of a subject will be altered under light of different wavelengths than those which it is structured to reflect. For this reason, television performers are usually lighted without the use of color filters over the light sources except for intentionally stylized effects.

4.2 The color of the subject is affected by the balancing of primary colors in the television system.

To understand more about the appearance of colors on television, it is useful to know something about the principle of additive color mixture, on which current television reproduction is based. You have probably observed that, when passed through a prism, white light separates into a rainbow-like spectrum of component hues. Vice versa, hues can be added together to constitute white light.

One way to do this is to use the three "light primaries," red, green and blue. When red, green and blue lights are added together, they will produce not only white light, but also (by varying their proportions) virtually every other hue. Therefore, they are used in the present color television system, both at the camera and the receiver end. The light entering the camera from the scene is separated into its component red, green and blue wavelengths, each component being directed to a separate pickup tube. In the receiver are three electron beams, one to respond to the output of each camera pickup tube. On the face of the receiver picture tube are particles called phosphors, grouped in triads—one phosphor in each triad glowing red, another green and another blue when activated by the relevant electron beam. Each triad combines the light from its phosphors to produce a bit of color corresponding to a tiny segment of the original scene.

The camera must be matched as closely as possible to the eye's relative sensitivity to various wavelengths. The eye is more sensitive to the yellow and green regions of the spectrum than to the red and blue regions. Adjusting the response of the camera to that of the eye is accomplished by proportioning or "balancing" the outputs of the red, green and blue pickup tubes. As a director, you must understand the need for this balancing and wait for it to be accomplished, allowing time for re-balancing just prior to the actual performance.

4.3 The color of the subject is affected by the camera's response to color temperature.

Camera balancing must take into account the color temperature, a term used to describe the relative proportion of the wavelengths in the illumination falling on the scene. In interior shots, for example, the blue tube output is increased to compensate for the relatively low blue content of incandescent light. If, meanwhile, another camera on the program is being used outdoors where there are more blue wavelengths in the natural light, it would require a different balance than the indoor camera. When these relative balances are accomplished, takes can be made between the two cameras without inconsistencies of color in successive shots.

Artificial light sources may differ in color temperature. Incandescent and fluorescent sources are too different in this respect to be mixed on the same subject without unpredictable results. Furthermore, color temperature changes when incandescent lights are dimmed, the filaments yielding progressively less blue and making skin tones brown, which leads some studios to set limits below which their lights should not be dimmed.

Natural light also varies in its constitution, being yellowish and reddish early and late in the day, blue in shade and overcast, and white in noon sunshine. As such changes occur, a filter can be used to change the quality of the light striking the pickup tubes to match that for which they are balanced. This adjustment may be needed during an outdoor remote which you are directing.

4.4   The color of the subject is adversely affected by too little illumination.

As previously mentioned, color requires a higher minimum level of scene brightness than monochrome television. A subject which is insufficiently lighted will not only fail to reveal its true color, but may also be mottled by spurious hues. For low key scenes (those in which dark tones predominate) light on the background must be kept relatively high.

4.5   The color of the subject is adversely affected by excessive contrast range.

For example, a camera takes a predominantly dark scene of three fashion models in royal blue ensembles, then zooms in to a closeup of a white bag which one of them is holding. As the iris (remotely controlled by the video engineer) is closed down to prevent overexposing the closeup, one can see the royal blue clothing darken to navy blue.

4.6   The color of the subject is affected by its reflective characteristics.

Thus, a wool and a satin may look different although colored by the same dye. Having a harder, smoother surface, the satin reflects some wavelengths which the wool absorbs and, acting more like a mirror, tends to reflect light beams in specific directions rather than to diffuse them, thus producing white highlights.

4.7   The color of the subject is influenced by the color of adjacent or background areas.

Flesh can be given a dark, muddy appearance from adjacency to excessively bright areas, including very light backgrounds, starchy white clothing and highly reflectant metals. To combat this, reflectant surfaces can be treated with a dulling spray.To darken a troublesome background, one may either move it farther from the light, angle it so that it reflects the light in a different direction, shield it from some of the light or re-aim the lighting instrument.

Flesh tones may change as they are seen in alternate shots against differently colored backgrounds. This effect is associated with a phenomenon called simultaneous hue contrast, whereby a color seen against some contrasting, highly saturated color, will take on some of the complement of that color. In light, the complement of a given hue is

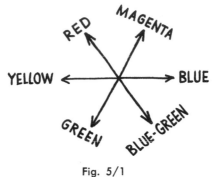

Fig. 5/1

the hue which, added to it, will produce white light. The hues opposite one another in *Figure 5/1* are complementary to each other. Note, for example, that the complement of yellow is blue, and that of blue-green is red. Therefore—illustrating the effect of simultaneous hue contrast—red raw beef on a yellow platter will take on blue (complement of the yellow), looking purplish and unappetizing, whereas on a blue-green platter its redness will be enhanced.

4.8   The color of the subject may be influenced by reflected light.

A subject may be colored by light which is reflected from a nearby colored surface or filtered through some nearby translucent material. For example, a face in the shadow of a tree may be green with light reflected from or filtered through the leaves, although this may be contrary to the viewer's expectations. Man tends to judge colors as he expects them to look and may regard as false the camera's objectivity.

4.9   The color of the subject may be affected by the performance of the color television system employed.

You may have to compensate for the characteristics of the particular system which you are using. One pioneer system, for example, tended to intensify red. Consequently, backlighted ears looked very red, indeed; a red boutonniere worn by a person in the background might be more evident than anything else in the picture; bright red lipstick and nail polish had to be avoided; in fact, the system prompted the development of a new line of makeup which was intentionally deficient in red. The system also intensified many other hues to the extent that costumes which were designed for stage spectacles proved too vivid for the television screen. The system also tended to reproduce gray and white with a bluish cast, so that faces, for example, had to be carefully powdered to prevent them from reflecting bluish glints. What is true of one system, however, may not be true of others, or even of the same system as it is improved by new engineering accomplishments.

Chapter 6

A Single Impression

In television, each new situation must be comprehended promptly before another replaces it. Hence, the visual elements which portray this situation must collaborate to produce a single, readily assimilated impression. Achieving this impression depends not only on what elements you select to show, but also on how you arrange them. In this arrangement, you seek to achieve unity through coherence and emphasis.

1   Work for coherent arrangements.

Coherence means "sticking together." In a coherent pictorial composition, the parts of the picture are visually connected so that they can be readily associated and grasped as a whole. In the interests of coherence:

1.1   Do not separate subjects on opposite sides of the picture.

To separate the subjects as in *Figure 6/1* splits the eye between two divergent centers of interest and provides nothing but emptiness in the center where one would expect the interest to be concentrated. So one sees:

ONE
PERSON

ANOTHER
PERSON

Fig. 6/1

whereas one should see:

TWO PERSONS UNITED
IN A CONVERSATION

Fig. 6/2

More involvement between the persons can be promoted by pulling the camera back. By introducing more space on either side of them, the space between them is relatively lessened, but the wider shot is liable to make them too small on the screen.

In *Figure 6/2,* the composition has been improved by moving the chairs closer together and by shooting from an angle to overlap the figures somewhat so that they tend to combine into a single visual form. As indicated by the arrows, a unified circular path has been established for the viewer's eyes.

1.2   Use scenic elements and lighting to tie the composition together.

In *Figure 6/3,* the men are as widely separated as in *Figure 6/1,* but the picture has been given more coherence by filling in between the men with scenic elements and light. The coffee table and its shadow bridge between the legs. The desk top forms a tie line at waist level. The books arch across above the heads. The lamp makes a center,

Fig. 6/3

holding the other elements by a kind of centripetal attraction, and the arc of light from it bridges between the faces.

1.3   Select a few expressive shapes and lines and repeat them, varied in size and direction, throughout the picture.

Because television directors work with living, moving subjects, they cannot observe as many niceties of coherence as are practiced by the designers of still pictures. Neverthless, for application to the relatively fixed compositions that occur in commercial displays or when performers remain stationary during a shot of appreciable duration, they will find the still picture composers' principles worthy of study.

One of these principles is to select a few expressive shapes and lines
and repeat them, varied in size and
direction, throughout the picture. In
Figure 6/4 (after a photograph advertising the insulation from noise
achieved by a brand of motor car
bodies), the sleeping child is arranged to emphasize gentle curves,
which repeat the curve formed by the
top of the car window and suggest
the caress of repose. The distribution

Fig. 6/4

of these curves throughout the picture gives coherence to its parts, making
them work together to produce a single, overall impression.

*1.4   Similarly in color television, repeat one or more hues, varied in
brightness and saturation, throughout the picture.*

Perhaps you already follow this principle in coordinating your attire or
the decoration of your room.

*1.5   Group smaller items into larger wholes that may be more easily
apprehended.*

This is similar to tying a number of small items into a bundle so that
they can be carried more easily. In writing, sentences are grouped into
paragraphs, paragraphs into sections, and sections into chapters, so that
ideas can be carried more conveniently in the mind. In pictorial composition, the separate visual elements are often grouped into embracing simple
geometric shapes.

For example, to correct the split attention which is evident in *Figure
6/5,* the performers in *Figure 6/6* have been grouped into a roughly triangular composition. This has been done by controlling the difference in head
levels and by coordinating the slants of the guitar, the girl's left arm, the
piano lid, and its supporting stick.

Figure 6/6 also demonstrates another means of helping the subject of

Fig. 6/5

Fig. 6/6

the picture to make a dominant impression. This is the calculated use of emphasis and subordination.

2   Emphasize picture elements in proportion to their importance.

The point of the picture statement in *Figure 6/6* is "girl singing." In supporting this point, the pictorial elements are not of equal importance. The piano and the guitar-playing accompanist are subordinate to the girl; and the girl's figure is subordinate to her face, which expresses her emotional attitude towards the song and contains the mouth from which the singing issues. Therefore, the face should receive more emphasis than anything else in the picture. Accordingly, it has been placed at the apex of the major triangle, with various slanting lines leading the eye to it. As the brightest element in the picture, juxtaposed against the darkest, it also commands attention by being at the point of highest brightness contrast.

You will not always find it as feasible to control emphasis as in this posed situation. Nevertheless, whatever the situation, you should see that those elements which carry the most meaning at any given moment command more attention than anything else in the frame.

The rest of this chapter cites ways to accomplish this objective. Although some of them have been mentioned before in this book, they are worth repeating.

2.1   *Frame as closely as possible around the meaningful elements.*

Beginning directors are apt to frame too loosely, showing, for example, a needlessly small human figure surrounded by a mass of background which has nothing to contribute to the matter at hand. You can, of course, include a wide expanse of background when it does mean something—if for instance, you want to contrast a small boy with the bigness of the world, or to support the lonesome mood of a ballad by surrounding the singer with empty space and shadow.

But sometimes not even a full figure should be framed. When the announcer of a cigarette commercial observes while exhaling, "You'll enjoy their cool, clean taste," the visual expression may be confined to his face, the cigarette at his lips and the exhaled smoke. A wider shot is justified in this instance only if something is to be gained by seeing his body in a supporting attitude of enjoyable relaxation—in which case it's up to you to make that attitude expressive enough to justify its inclusion in the picture.

2.2   *When small subjects must share the screen with human beings, bring them as close as possible to the performers' faces.*

Suppose that an announcer, saying, "Acme is the key to your security," holds a key at waist level, thereby requiring you to frame him in a hip shot. In this shot, the small size of the key and the number of other visual elements with which it must compete for attention do not make the key as visually assertive as it should be. By having the announcer raise the key nearer his face and extend it somewhat towards camera, you can take a tighter shot in which the key will gain its due prominence.

When small items are being demonstrated on a table surface, there are two possible ways to bring them closer to the demonstrator's face: you can lower the person by seating him—or, if he must remain standing, you can raise the table surface, choosing a waist-level counter, for example, instead of a standard height table.

2.3 To make small subjects dominate larger ones, place them in the foreground of the shot.

Note, for example, the location of the telephone in *Figure 4/12.*

2.4 Elongated subjects may require special composition to make them dominate the picture.

When shot from front and center, a vocal chorus three tiers deep and twenty persons wide will have to compete for visual attention with large, meaningless areas of floor at the bottom of the picture or of background at the top. To make it fill more of the frame, you can either:

. . . regroup it in more vertical tiers with fewer persons per row (provided that it can still sing well in this arrangement), or

. . . shoot it from an angle, which will compress its pictured width, or

. . . shoot it from above, which will make it fill more of the height of the screen by revealing more of the bodies of persons in the second and third tiers than could be seen in a lower shot.

A cigarette carton can present similar problems. Instead of shooting it from front and center as in *Figure 6/7,* try taking it as in *Figure 6/8* from an angle high enough to show its top as well as its face, also slanting it to

Fig. 6/7

Fig. 6/8

cut across more of the vertical dimension of the frame. Projecting a shadow from it may also help to extend the influence of the carton over more of the picture area.

2.5   Contrast the important element with its environment.

Slanting the carton as in *Figure 6/8* also makes it more prominent by contrast with the rectangular alignment of the picture frame.

In *Figure 6/6*, the prominence of the girl vocalist was also achieved partly by contrast. Observe that her figure, as the only vertical in the picture, contrasts in direction with the other major lines. Also, as previously noted, the maximum brightness contrast is between the dark piano cover and her face.

Contrast can be useful for emphasizing a commercial product. For example, a smooth-surfaced container will be more assertive when displayed against a textured surface.

Various kinds of possible contrast are listed below:

Standing	Seated	Diagonal	Rectangular
Tall	Low	Flat	In the round
Small	Large	Alone	Together
Bright	Dark	Moving	Still
Distant	Close	Detailed	Plain
Focused	Blurred	Contrasty	Uniform
Curved	Straight	Rough	Smooth

And in color television, you may also contrast warm colors with cool colors, a saturated color with a desaturated one, and a given hue with its complementary hue.

2.6   Lead towards the important elements with lines to be traveled by the eye.

In *Figure 6/6* you have already noted how various diagonals lead towards the singer's face at the apex of the major triangle. Various printings also demonstrate how the center of interest can be emphasized by placing it where prominent lines converge. In Leonardo da Vinci's "Last Supper," for example, the head of Jesus coincides with the vanishing point of all receding lines in the composition.

In advertising layouts, lines serve not only to control the eye's path through the message, but also to keep it from wandering off into adjacent copy. Similarly, you should avoid compositions which pull your viewer's eye away from the center of interest. Avoid, for example, the arrangement in *Figure 4/6* (page 34), where attention is led back and off the screen by the perspective convergence of the display board and by the direction in which the teacher is facing. Obviously, the direction in which your performers face can and should be used to support the center of interest.

2.7 Make the important elements more visibly communicative than other elements.

When two or more performers are included in the frame, attention is likely to center on the one who is most actively communicating, whether by speech or movement. This obviously requires that sound and motion by the supporting characters be subordinated to that of the one who is leading the scene at a given moment.

In dialogue passages where no performer is particularly more active than another, attention will favor the one whose features are most clearly revealed. If two persons are facing camera at different distances from it— all else being equal—the one closer to camera is likely to be more prominent because his face is larger and is resolved in greater detail. If they are facing each other, however, more prominence will attach to the one farther from camera because more of his features are revealed.

2.8 To achieve proper emphasis, control the brightness levels.

Avoid painting or lighting the background so brightly that it dominates the persons in front of it, who, almost ten times out of ten, are more important than it is.

Avoid overhead lighting which shadows the performers' eyes, frustrating the attention which should be given to these "mirrors of the soul."

Study how artists like Goya and Rembrandt brighten their center of interest or reinforce it with the strongest brightness contrast in their picture.

Experiment with light as a means to shift attention from one center of attention to another, either by moving performers in and out of shadow, or by dimming the light on one subject and bringing it up on another.

2.9 Simplify the environment of the important element, eliminating items which would compete with it for attention.

When a demonstrator is showing a sucession of items, keep the display surface clear of other items than the one which is important at the moment. This may require an adjacent area from which the items can be procured and another to which they can be removed. Shooting downwards towards

Fig. 6/9

the display surface will help to eliminate the body of the demonstrator from the closeup.

If several objects are to be panned in sequence, they should be spaced sufficiently apart so that only one appears on camera at a time.

Avoid busy backgrounds. These include not only the vertical surfaces of the setting, but also the clothing of demonstrators. For example, it is difficult to discern a fountain pen sufficiently if it is being held in front of a checked suit. Sometimes the demonstrator can hold the item to one side of him so that his body does not appear in the closeup at all.

3   When choosing a lens for a given shot, consider what emphasis you desire.

Your choice of a lens can determine how much larger one subject appears than another, and also which subjects are in focus and which ones are not.

3.1   Emphasis is affected by the depth of field.

When two subjects are at different distances from camera, you can give them equal emphasis by keeping them both in sharp focus. For this you will need ample depth of field.

But to focus more sharply on one than the other, you will need limited

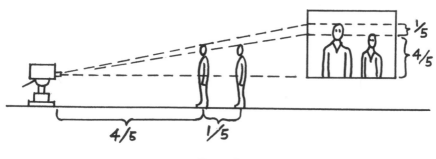

Fig. 6/10

depth of field. When taking closeups of single items, it is usually desirable to make them stand out against a softer focused background. This is more easily achieved by using a lens of relatively long focal length.

3.2   When two subjects are at different distances from camera, the difference in size between them can be increased by using a shorter lens, with the camera in close..

See *Figures 6/9* and *6/10*. In *Figure 6/9* the rear subject is twice as far from the camera as the front subject; hence he looks only half as large. But in *Figure 6/10* the subjects are separated by only one fifth of the total distance from the camera to the rear subject; hence the rear subject appears only one fifth smaller than the one in front.

In both instances the figure in front is framed at the waist. In *Figure 6/9* this is accomplished with a lens of short focal length, in *Figure 6/10* by a lens of longer focal length.

If domination by size is desired, clearly one should select the lens of short focal length, which increases the difference in scale by requiring that the camera be brought in close.

By lowering the camera, incidentally, the dominance of the nearer subject can be further increased, since the lower the camera, the taller the nearer subject will appear in relation to the farther one.

Chapter 7

Distractions and Discomforts

A viewer is less likely to heed the point of a picture statement if something about it distracts him or makes him feel uncomfortable. Therefore:

1   Take pains with your picture composition.

1.1   Pay attention to balance, particularly when your subjects are in relatively fixed positions.

The principles of balance as practiced by painters are applicable in television mainly to static situations, but there are more of such situations than one may at first realize, for the motion of performers often consists of transitions between tableaux which are held for moments at a time.

When a picture is unbalanced, the elements which attract greatest attention seem to predominate on one side of it, making the other side seem wasted. High attention goes naturally to persons who are doing or saying something or to persons and things which are being talked about, but attention is also inflenced by other factors such as size, color, and contrast. Attention factors can interact in complex ways. A tiny highlight against a dark background can balance a large mass of middle gray, or a top spinning on a bare floor can balance a whole group of boys watching it. All of the various interest values in the picture average out at some spot which resembles a center of gravity. When this center is felt to be nearer one side of the picture than the other, the picture is unbalanced.

1.2   Place attractions of equal attention value equidistant from the center.

This is called symmetrical balance or symmetry. It is similar in principle to placing persons of equal weight equidistant from the fulcrum of a seesaw.

1.3   When attractions are unequal, the stronger should be nearer the center on its side of the picture.

This is asymmetrical balance or asymmetry. It resembles balancing a seesaw by seating the heavier person nearer the fulcrum and the lighter farther from it.

1.4   In some instances, balance for television differs from that for still pictures.

A performer looking off-screen should be framed with more room on the side towards which he is looking; this balances off audience interest in whatever is attracting his attention. Similarly, when panning with a laterally moving subject, a cameraman customarily leads the subject, allowing more room on the side towards which he is moving. Although, as previously explained, this is done partly to prevent the subject from intersecting with the frame in case of an unexpected spurt, it also serves to balance off the interest which has been created in the subject's destination.

When two performers, A and B, who are conversing, are taken separately in alternate shots, it is customary to frame A with more room on the side off which B is located, and B with more room on the side off which A is located. Not only does this compensate for off-screen interest as explained above, but it also keeps each performer on that side of the screen which he is seen to occupy when the two are taken together, thus preventing a disturbing spatial disorientation.

When a picture is unbalanced, the viewer instinctively wants to see the wasted side filled with something. Capitalizing on this, a director will sometimes unbalance his composition intentionally to create anticipation for something which he is about to introduce on the empty side. Thus, actors may be moved away from a door just before the entrance of an important character; or the camera may pan a commercial product to one side of the screen, creating on the other side a kind of vacuum, which will be filled presently with an important printed message.

1.5   Prevent the following instances of faulty composition or poor framing:

There is too much headroom. The performer has sunk too low in the picture, leaving the upper part to no purpose.

There is too little headroom. The performer's head is scraping the top of the frame.

The performer is cut off at the ankles as if wading or soaking his feet.

The corner of a picture frame on the wall behind a performer looks as if it might puncture his head.

A lampshade or plant rises behind a performer's head like an exotic headdress.

In the shot of a panelist, halves of other panelists' bodies are seen moving on either side of the frame.

A very white and very unimportant piece of paper—or in color television, a red carnation in an announcer's buttonhole—is the most apparent object in the shot.

The hands of a performer are moving just below the frame so that one can't make out what they are doing.

. . . The foregoing are only the beginning of a list to which you are urged to add your own examples. Then you can say, as in *The Mikado,* "I've got them on the list, and they'll none of them be missed."

2   Help performers to avoid inappropriate action or unattractive appearance.

2.1   When the performer is supposed to be addressing the audience, help him to make eye contact with the lens.

So that the performer will not have to look off camera for his starting cue, be sure that the floor director who gives the cue stations himself alongside the opening camera.

So that the performer will not be caught with an "I'm taking a cue" look when the camera dissolves to him, your direction should be, "Mike, cue, dissolve"—not "Mike, dissolve, cue him."

Inexperienced performers never seem to be really talking to the audience when they are trying to read prompting devices (except, perhaps, for the kind that projects the copy on a glass directly in front of the lens). Encourage them, therefore, to speak from their own knowledge, referring frankly to notes when they come to data which the audience would not expect them to remember anyway. Unless they are able to sustain long speeches straight from their own minds, provide someone who, by asking leading questions, can prompt the information from them a little at a time. If they cannot do without a prompting device, pray that they are far-sighted. This will allow you to keep the camera back from them on a narrow-angle lens, thus reducing the number of degrees through which they must move their eyes off-lens to read the copy.

Be sure the performer knows which camera he is supposed to be talking to. It is not always easy for him to judge this for himself. For example, if he is pointing out details in a diagram hung at eye level, both the camera taking the closeup of the diagram and the camera which includes his face will be aimed at approximately the same level and in approximately the same direction.

Also be sure that the camera he is supposed to address is located where he can do so conveniently. In *Figures 7/1* and *7/2,* a performer is pointing out details in a diagram, taken in closeup by camera 2, which leaves 1 as the camera to take his face whenever he seeks to direct a remark to his viewers. In *Figure 7/1* he can do this conveniently—but in *Figure 7/2,* note how he can do so only by twisting his head awkwardly over his shoulder, since camera 1, unhappily, is precisely where many beginning directors are liable to locate it.

Fig. 7/1

Fig. 7/2

2.2   When a performer is addressing the television audience, refrain from changing cameras during his speech.

Otherwise, he may jerk his head noticeably from one camera to the other. If the change is unavoidable, the performer should be trained, when noticing the tally light go out on the first camera, to glance momentarily towards some intermediate center of attention before looking into the second camera.

2.3   Eliminate unsightly parts of performers' bodies.

Closeups of table-top demonstrations should avoid giving undue prominence to the pelvic region of the demonstrator behind the table.

It is remarkable what a confusion of angles can be assumed by the legs of a seated group of persons, and how distracting these legs can be, particularly if they are female. For masking these distractions no studio should be without a coffee table.

2.4   Eliminate annoying factors about the performers' grooming and dress.

Among these are shiny tie clips, dangling earrings that sway in closeups, and sometimes open zipper plackets.

2.5   Eliminate distasteful business.

In a student-directed commercial, a young lady serving iced tea dropped ice cubes into the glass with her fingers and then wiped the fingers on her apron. The director seemed not to notice.

2.6   Correct movements which are awkward or distracting.

For example, a performer may keep swaying back and forth in a closeup. He may keep repeating some physical mannerism. Or he may be ungainly when sitting and rising—possibly because the director has settled for a seat that is too low, deep and soft.

2.7   Do what you can to prevent nervous tension.

Inexperienced performers need orientation to the studio techniques and role expected of them. They should not be expected to take cues, regulate the timing and progress of the program, sustain a lengthy presentation, perform intricate business, deliver imposed speeches requiring memorization, or, in short, do anything to which they are unaccustomed.

The director should allow every performer the freest possible exercise of his own individual faculties of communication. Find out whether he is more comfortable sitting or standing. Don't confuse him with a barrage of instructions. Don't inhibit him with too many restrictions as to where to stand, how to hold things, which camera to play to, etc., until he is ready to accommodate himself to these restrictions. A person under tension in a strange situation can take only so much at one time.

3 Be alert to correct discomforts and distractions caused by scenery, properties and graphics.

These include:

Unpressed cloths   Amateurish lettering
Badly draped drapes   Cracks between flats
Wrinkled cycloramas   Shaking walls
Bruised or dirty surfaces   Askew pictures

4 Prevent disturbances caused by faulty lighting.

4.1 Prevent visible shadow of the microphone boom.

To do this, keep performers away from the walls of the setting as much as possible.

Provide the lighting crew with advance information about the area to be covered by your boom microphone and about the locations, facing directions, and movements of your performers and cameras.

Be willing to entertain recommendations from the lighting people regarding the best location for your boom. The more perpendicular it is to the direction of predominant spotlight beams, the less liable it will be to project vertical shadows on the walls and on the performers' bodies. Horizontal shadows are much easier to mask out than vertical ones; they can often be eliminated by lowering the top "barn door" on the spotlight which is causing the trouble.

4.2 Do not tolerate multiple shadows of a subject, except for a desired special effect.

These are particularly obvious and distracting when made by a moving subject.

4.3 Do not tolerate unattractive shadows on performers, such as:

. . . those which do not conform to the natural contours of the face, as when nose shadow drops onto the upper lip.

. . . those from strong toplight, which obscure the eyes and throw unnatural emphasis on the horizontal planes of the face.

. . . those from excessive backlight, which make "bibs" on the chest.

. . . those which are too dark and hard-edged, particularly on an attractive female face.

. . . those which create unmotivated dark pockets in the space through which performers move.

4.4   Prevent glare.

This results when a light beam is reflected from a bright or glossy surface directly towards the camera lens. To correct it, several remedies are possible.

The surface can be altered to provide diffuse reflection (which scatters rays in many different directions) instead of specular reflection (which reflects the beam in one primary direction). For instance, a shiny object can be sprayed with dulling wax, or matte photographs can be substituted for glossy ones.

The light falling on the surface can be made more diffuse, either by flooding out a spotlight beam, or by using a scoop instead of a spotlight, or by placing a diffusing medium in front of the instrument, or by caroming the light off some intermediate diffusing surface rather than turning it directly onto the shiny object.

The angle of the troublesome surface can be changed so that it does not reflect the beam towards the camera lens. For example, when holding glossy photographs, performers can incline them slightly downward, thereby directing the reflected beam beneath the lens. In applying this remedy, remember the law from your physics textbook: "The angle of incidence equals the angle of reflection."

The camera can be moved out of the path of the reflected light beam.

4.5   Prevent multiple light reflections.

Large reflectant subjects such as motor cars will not look well if they reflect multiple bright images of the studio lights. Besides glaring, these multiple highlights can look unnatural, be unduly prominent, and break up the subject's unity of form. To correct them, apply some of the remedies suggested for correcting glare--or try using one or two powerful light sources instead of several weaker ones, thus producing fewer reflected beams for the camera to have to avoid.

4.6   *Prevent halation.*

Arcs of spurious light will wash in from one edge of the picture when the camera faces unshielded light sources which are just outside its field of view. If, as often happens, it is backlights which cause this problem, either raise them or use barndoors to mask off their beams from the camera lens.

5   Prevent spurious electronic effects.

Certain undesirable effects appear on the screen when production conditions are unfavorable in some manner to the electronic system, particularly to the type of camera pickup tube which is being used. Different types of tubes are subject to different effects. Some of the effects have been greatly minimized by new tube designs. However, you may encounter as of this writing:

5.1   *Image retention, memory or burn-in*

The image of a subject which has occupied a fixed location on the screen remains visible after the camera has been trained on a different subject. This condition is aggravated by the age of the tube and the degree of contrast in the subject. Bright highlights will burn in readily and be especially noticeable. On some cameras the condition is counteracted by orbitors, which keep the image rotating almost imperceptibly on the tube face. Lacking these, when a shot remains static for a time, the director may need to have the cameraman pan or tilt very, very slowly, or dolly very slowly in and out.

5.2   *Smear or lag*

A trail is perceived behind the subject when the camera or the subject moves rapidly. This is caused by the phosphors in some kinds of tubes continuing to glow over long after the stimulus has ceased.

5.3   *Black halo*

A smudge appears around the images of excessively bright subjects such as exposed flames or highly reflectant metals.

5.4   *I.O. (Image Orthicon) ghost*

Excessively bright subjects give rise to nebulous secondary images of themselves, displaced somewhat from the primary image. These are especially evident in dark areas, as when a white breast pocket handkerchief is ghosted on a dark dinner jacket.

5.5   Streaking

Streaks may project across the picture from such subjects as lettering, the slats of Venetian blinds, and the edges of shelves when these are very contrasty and run horizontally on the screen. They can be prevented by reducing the contrast and by shooting troublesome scenic items from an angle so that their images will slant on the screen.

5.6   "The beat"

At certain distances from camera, narrow, contrasty checks and patterns such as that in houndstooth suiting material will cause an effect like heat waves rising or rippling moiré silk.

5.7   Fogging or mottling

Cloudy patches can result from various causes, including certain malfunctions of the system. The patches will be particularly evident in large, evenly toned areas, especially dark ones. The more variety of tone and detail in the picture, the greater chance there is of the mottling going unnoticed.

6   Do what you can to eliminate poor camerawork.

It is obvious that discomfort and distraction will result from:

. . . failures to maintain focus and framing,

. . . camera movements which are not motivated by program content,

. . . jerky or wavering pans and dollies,

. . . lurching zooms,

. . . shooting off the set,

. . . showing an overhead microphone, unless its presence has been frankly acknowledged,

. . . and late shots.

All of these the director must be ever watchful to correct or to prevent. You cannot always count on having expert camera operators. You may have to spend some of your directing time teaching them composition, timing, and camera handling techniques.

Chapter 8

Animation or Liveliness

A shot can be clear, recognizable, emphatic, and free from distractions, yet fail to interest the viewer because it is visually monotonous. Therefore:

1 Provide a variety of brightness levels.

Just as you feel more alert on a sunny day than an overcast one, your viewer will respond more alertly to a television picture with some snap in it. In monochrome television, the lack of color variety should be compensated for by adequate gray-scale variety, including small accents of the brightest and darkest tones which the system can reproduce. These accents not only liven up the picture, but also serve as reference levels which help the engineers to establish proper gradations between the intermediate tones.

To achieve sufficient tonal variety in monochrome, choose colors for scenery, wearing apparel, and properties which will reproduce in clearly differentiated gray-scale steps ranging from a fairly dark to a fairly light gray, reserving black and white for small accenting touches. If the colors you must work with seem too monotonous in monochrome under even illumination, use modeling light to add highlights and shadows. For the snap and sparkle of highlights in eyes and on the summits of facial contours, use spotlights rather than sources of diffuse illumination.

2   Provide a variety of size and spacing.

Arrange your performers at different heights on the screen and at different distances from camera. Avoid equal spaces between them except for an intentionally formal effect.

In general, prefer asymmetrical to symmetrical compositions. Symmetry is justified when you intend a formal effect, or when you wish to give equal importance to two participants who are sharing a scene, or when you need to give equal treatment to a row of singers or dancers who are all doing the same thing. But don't cultivate the habit of shooting everything from front and center. There are more ways to shoot the news announcer than to frame him between balanced pictures on the wall behind him and balanced desk pens on the desk in front of him. Such regularity is trite, unimaginative, and too inanimate to reflect life as most of us experience it.

3   Use the dynamic potential of the diagonal.

Picture designers often seek to affect their viewers by the direction they give to prominent lines in their compositions. Long, horizontal lines are used to induce a feeling of repose. Diagonals, on the other hand, engender a sense of excitement and activity. In television, diagonals can be used to animate shots which lack actual motion. For example, compare *Figures 6/7* and *6/8* (page 63). It is probable that you will respond more alertly to the slanted carton than to the horizontal one.

4   Encourage the animation and naturalness of your performers.

Give your performers opportunity to move around a little rather than freezing them too long or too rigidly in blocked-out positions.

When they do remain in one location, let them assume as natural and informal a pose as possible unless you have good reason for the contrary. Avoid head-on full shots of seated persons with their knees pointed straight towards camera unless you want to make them look like old Egyptian statues. Let them sit with their bodies slanted to camera. Besides looking more natural and comfortable that way, they'll fill out the width of the screen better than when forming a narrow perpendicular straight up and down the middle of it.

Chapter 9

Expressiveness

Last but not least in the Moment-by-Moment Questionnaire, you should ask: "Does my picture express the meaning as effectively as it should? Does it convey the desired character and mood?" To insure that it does, ask these further questions:

1 What part of the subject should I show?

Have I restricted my shot to that part of the scene which makes the point most effectively? A common error is to show too much, to diffuse the attention over things that don't matter. Get in on what counts.

Sometimes it is better to leave something to the imagination. A student director showed his understanding of this principle (although perhaps no great originality) when, after establishing a boy overwhelming a girl with an ardent embrace, he cut away to show a cigarette dropping from her hand unheeded.

Details are sometimes more eloquent than generalities. Hands or feet may be more expressive than faces. And reactions may occasionally mirror an event with more impact than provided by a view of the event itself.

2 What camera angle should I use?

Shooting up from a low angle is commonly used to give the subject dominance and power; shooting down, to make it seem weak and inferior—or to identify the viewer with a superior position.

Some subjects make sense only from a high angle—for example, a bowl of soup, a phonograph record or certain square dance patterns. With some subjects the angle depends on your purpose: you shoot a bowl on the level when stressing its profile as characteristic of a particular art style, but from overhead if interested in its contents.

There is always a best angle from which to show such operations as working at looms, operating sewing machines, making block prints, etc. If you have to determine the angle before actually seeing the operation, it pays to find out whether the operator is right- or left-handed; otherwise, you may have to completely reverse your set-up. If the television viewer is expected to be able to copy the process being demonstrated, try to show him the materials as he will face them when he tries the process for himself.

Some dramatic segments employ subjective camera angles: the camera assumes the point of view of one of the characters so that the viewer will identify more closely with his experience. This technique usually requires that the shooting be stopped while the camera is placed in the character's position. Hence it is feasible only when recording in segments on film or video tape which can subsequently be edited together.

3   What framing—loose or tight?

Sometimes you need to get very close to details which make the points most strongly: glaring eyes, beads of sweat on a brow or the flying fingers of a pianist during a nimble passage. In this latter case, the closer the fingers, the more their changing angles will contrast with the fixed margins of the frame, thus making them seem to fly even faster.

Shoot loose, however, when the environment adds meaning to the shot. An expanse of bookshelves may reinforce the authority of a learned person. The shadowy space of an empty house may add suspense. Or the space left in front of a crippled child who is walking for the first time without his crutch may add more impact to his achievement.

4   What perspective?

Perspective can be varied by your choice of lens. For example, an extreme wide-angle lens can be used to:

    . . . distort facial closeups for a grotesque or comic effect.

    . . . increase the apparent force of a blow delivered towards camera.

. . . intensify the speed and enlargement of persons or vehicles moving towards the camera, being even more effective sometimes when used from a low camera position.

. . . increase the difference in scale between a subject in the foreground and one farther away.

. . . add apparent depth to a room or increase the apparent length of an automobile which is angled towards the camera.

. . . make a small subject in the foreground dominate a larger one in the background.

5 What focus?

Soft focus is sometimes used to disguise the lines on a face which has passed its bloom. It can help to create a romantic mood. It can dematerialize the background in a scene which depends more upon feeling or spirit than upon clear perception of physical material, such as poetry readings or a minister's sermon. By soft focusing what doesn't matter, you can make what does matter assert itself more positively.

6 What lighting quality—hard or soft?

Hard lighting, showing abrupt transitions between strongly contrasting highlights and shadows, is appropriate for action which contains sudden reversals, striking surprises, intense climaxes, and boldly delineated characters. It is produced by focused spotlights, aimed at an angle to the camera, with little diffuse light to soften the shadows.

Soft lighting—used for gentler and less dramatic action—has limited contrast and gradual transitions between highlights and shadows. For this, the spotlights are flooded out, and scoops with diffusion media are used for fill light, to dilute the shadows.

7 What lighting—high or low key?

Most programs are played in the relatively even, bright-appearing illumination known as "high key." Night scenes or somber ones use "low key," which simulates low illumination. "Simulates" is used advisedly for, as mentioned in Chapter 4, the video engineer will object to dimming all the lights on the scene. He needs enough illumination to prevent a noisy picture. He needs some highlights as "reference whites" to help him establish the proper levels of other tones.

High key is not achieved simply by turning on more and more light. As the light is increased, the lenses will have to be stopped down to keep some of it from entering the camera; and light which does not enter the camera goes wasted. Besides, the light will seem bright only when there are dark tones present to contrast with it. If the performers' faces do not seem bright enough, the solution may be not to add more light to them, but rather to gain more contrast by reducing the background illumination. This remedy will also save some electrical power.

8 What linear composition?

A model who bends her wrist and elbow in sharp angles will add little grace or salesmanship to a commercial for beauty aids, nor will a display of such products if it is composed primarily in rectangles.

Lines stimulate different responses depending on their direction and configuration. Vertical lines are generally used to denote strength and stability—or if very high, aspiration; horizontals are used for calm and repose; diagonals for activity; zigzags for excitement; plump curves for affluence; gently flowing curves for grace.

Study the use of lines in painting. For example, observe how Fragonard uses curves for grace and voluptuousness in "The Bathers" and how Titian lends acuity to his sitter's character by the acute angles in his "Man With Glove."

9 What color?

This question, of course, applies to color television. That colors can symbolize meanings and stimulate emotional reactions seems evident, but much that has been stated on this subject is speculative. The matter is complicated, since the effect will differ depending on whether a hue is dull or intense, light or dark. It will also depend on what colors are combined in a given scheme. Thus, the juxtaposition of intense complementaries such as red and blue-green will be more exciting than an arrangement of analogous hues such as blue and violet; and even more sedate will be the monochromatic scheme in which a single hue is varied in saturation and brightness, as when orange is modified to produce harmonies in tan and brown. Furthermore, the effects of color vary with the sex, health, age, nationality, associations and other characteristics of the beholder, making generalizations unreliable.

Nevertheless, many works on color assign "feelings" to the various hues. For example,

Red:	exciting, fervid, active
Orange:	lively, energetic, forceful
Yellow:	cheerful, inspiring, vital
Green:	peaceful, quieting, refreshing
Blue:	subduing, sober
Purple:	dignified, mournful
White:	pure, clean, youthful
Black:	ominous, deadly, depressing

Use such tables at your own discretion.

10　What physical relationships between the performers?

Whether characters face or shun each other, whether they are distant or close, whether one is higher than another or on the same level—such physical relationships are one of the dramatic director's principle means of expression, as you can learn by consulting books about directing for the theater.

In non-dramatic programs, too, the physical relationship between performers can be used to express their intellectual or emotional relationship. For example, participants in a public affairs program who represent opposing views will seem to be more in conflict if they confront each other across some separating space or person than if they are seated side by side. In a quiz show, panelists on the same team would logically be adjacent to one another and facing in the same direction, whereas the moderator would be distinguished from them by being assigned a separate location.

Chapter 10

Keeping Up With the Action

In the preceding seven chapters you have been concerned with the appearance of the television picture as if halted at a given moment. But a program consists of many successive moments and many changing pictures. The arrangement of pictures in time sequence is often referred to as pictorial continuity.

Continuity means that something keeps going without interruption. The important thing to keep going without interruption is your viewer's absorption in the program. He should remain immersed in the program content, moving from one picture statement to another with no obstacles to his concentration or understanding.

He should not be perplexed by failing to understand how each new picture he sees is related to those which preceded it.

He should not be distracted from the content to the technical means or "mechanics" by which the content is communicated.

He should not be frustrated by not being shown what he wants to see when he wants to see it.

These last three sentences provide the subjects for the chapters that you will read next. In this chapter you are going to consider the third sentence and the rule that follows from it:

1 Show what your viewer wants to see when he wants to see it.

To do this, you must be ready to show each event as it happens. Hence, you must have your cameras in the right place at the right time. In terms of the trade, you are "hung" when the only available camera is unable to get the shot you need. This situation may be due to any of several reasons. The camera may be in the wrong place, or aimed in the wrong direction, or on the wrong lens—and time may be too short to right these wrongs.

But the wrongs should never have occurred in the first place, had the camerawork been planned correctly. In this chapter, therefore, you will find a number of recommendations for keeping your cameras ready to take the action as it occurs. The first of these recommendations is:

2 Plan your shot alternation before coming to the studio.

In *Figure 10/1,* camera 1 is logically situated to take the last shot of the master of ceremonies as he cues a dissolve into closing captions on the title drum—but camera 2 is in no position to get that next shot of the drum. To avoid such predicaments, plan your camera treatment in advance, dovetailing shots and action so that each time a particular subject needs to be shown, the camera which can show it best is always available.

Fig. 10/1

3 Remember your camera plan.

Having made your camera plan, be sure that you have it so clearly in mind that, while calling the shots, you can readily remember what is supposed to happen next and call for it without causing any delays yourself. The more you depend upon reading your script, the more liable you are to lose your place in it, and the more you must take your attention away from a critical inspection of the pictures and sound that are telling your story on the air.

4   Make sure that the cameramen and performers understand your plan.

4.1   Have them demonstrate that they do.

The best assurance that they do understand is to have them demonstrate the desired action during rehearsal. Then you'll *know* there is time enough for the camera to move to its new position, for instance, and that the cameraman understands what this position is to be.

4.2   When rehearsal is short, at least rehearse the more critical and difficult maneuvers.

Walk the performers through any major changes of position while the cameramen try following them. Know in advance which effects you must devote your time to and how much time to allow for each. Don't become so immersed in perfecting one of them that you rob time from the others.

4.3   If there's no rehearsal, brief the cameramen in advance.

Catch them when you can to prepare them for difficult maneuvers: "You'll be boomed down on Betsy, seated behind her desk. Then you'll boom up as she rises, dolly back diagonally to your left as she comes forward to the pedestal, ending wide enough to let in her guest and favor him; he'll be standing at the left of the pedestal. Think you can find a minute to practice it before air time?" Hopefully he will, since he doesn't want a reputation for sloppy camerawork; and even if the performers aren't present, he can practice in relation to the furniture.

4.4   Prepare shot sheets.

When shots promise to come too thick and fast for adequate verbal explanation during the program, you can prepare a shot sheet to be taped to the back of each camera for the cameraman to read. Here are two core-lated examples:

CAMERA 1	CAMERA 2
Shot #	Shot #
1 Title on easel.	2 CU host (left chair) Dolly back into 2-shot.
3 CU guest (rt. chair)	4 Same; pan them to pedestal.
5 Waist shot of guest & trophy on pedestal.	6 Both, with trophy, at pedestal
7 CU trophy.	

. . . and so on.

4.5   Explain, when necessary, from the studio floor.

You can expedite some matters by explaining them, not from the control room, but from the studio floor, where you can actually point out locations and demonstrate positions without having to describe them through the studio loudspeaker or through the floor director, which can sometimes be a difficult and time-wasting procedure. While working on the floor, you can ask someone back in the control room to punch up the shots for your inspection on the studio monitor.

5   Before the actual performance, make sure that things are restored to their opening positions.

Ascertain that cards are restacked in the correct order on easels, film re-cued, slide projectors re-set, properties back in their proper places, so that the right subject will be in the right place at the right time.

6   When shooting ad-lib, keep a cover shot.

Some shows, of course, cannot be rehearsed. In a ball game or a panel show, for instance, you will know the general pattern of the action, but you cannot predict the specific sequence in which it will develop. Nevertheless, you will need some overall plan which will let you show the unexpected when it occurs.

When action is ad lib and you yourself cannot get a good view of it, you may wish to let a cameraman find his own shots, hoping thereby to catch colorful bits of human interest or unanticipated fast developments. Beware, however, lest all of your cameras get frozen on closeups so that none is available for some important occurrence elsewhere in the scene. It is prudent to reserve one camera for cover shots, shots which show the total situation. Then, when the unexpected occurs, you can take the cover shot until you have time to swing another camera over for a closer look at the situation.

Incidentally, make it clear in advance whether you do want a cameraman to find his own shots or to wait for your directions. Otherwise, he may wander off a shot which you were planning to return to and thus leave you in trouble.

7   Assign areas of responsibility.

It is sometimes advisable to assign to each cameraman a specific area of responsibility beyond which he should not stray. In covering a baseball game, for instance, one camera may be responsible for the pitcher's delivery to the batter, another (on a wide lens) to establish where the hit goes, and a third to take a close shot of the ball being fielded, etc.

A similar arrangement can be made with your cameramen in studio situations such as the round-table discussion that is diagrammed in *Figure 10/2*. Camera 1 is assigned to take the chairman and occasional shots of the total group. Camera 2 is responsible for panelist B, and camera 3 for panelist D. When either 2 or 3 is not feeding program, it is responsible for panelist C. For example, D has been speaking on camera 3. If C speaks next, it is camera 2's responsibility to get him. On the other hand, if B has been speaking on camera 2, and then C speaks, it is camera 3's responsibility to get C. If D should then interrupt, camera 3 will pan from C to D. This plan will work with maximum efficiency if the panelists are required to signal and be acknowledged by the chairman before speaking, thus giving the cameramen advance notice about which panelist they are to frame next.

Fig. 10/2

8   Try to eliminate extra-quick shot changes.

During continuous sequences of action, it can take a substantial length of time to get the next shot ready. For example, while camera 1 is feeding its signal, the director considers his next subject, then says, "2, on the little girl's face." Then the operator of camera 2 has to find the little girl, pan to her, change lenses, move his dolly to adjust his framing, and focus his lens. Not until then can the director say, "Take 2."

Realize, therefore, that you cannot expect to change shots as quickly as in some edited film sequences. This is particularly true in unrehearsed productions. However, you can speed up your shot changes by observing some of the following recommendations when you are planning your camera set-up.

9   Arrange for a sequence of subjects to be shot in the same location.

A cameraman can find his next shot quickly if his subjects follow one another in the same location. For demonstrations, therefore, it is often advisable to have but a single area on which the camera assigned to closeups is trained and where materials are shown one after another. Sometimes the material can be rolled past the camera on castored stands, or placed around the circumference of a round table which revolves like a "lazy Susan" past the lens.

Similarly, it is helpful to concentrate pictures, charts and other graphics in a single area. Thus, the rectangular opening shown in *Figure 10/3* is designed to hold either a stack of opaque cards or a rear projection screen on which a series of slides can be shown. The revolving cubes in *Figure 10/4* can bring before camera four different surfaces, which may include a chalkboard, magnetic board or cork boards for mounting picture displays.

Fig. 10/3   Fig. 10/4

Such concentrated areas minimize the delays and possible errors caused by having to move the camera between shots. They also conserve studio space and restrict the area which needs to be lighted.

10   Minimize unnecessary camera movement.

10.1   Find base positions from which cameras can command a maximum variety of shots without needless adjustments.

Unless camera rehearsal time is generous, minimize camera movement except when it is necessary for an intended effect. Obviously, you may want to dolly in to support a climax, or dolly out to admit new subject matter, or pan with a moving performer. But you will not want to move your cameras unnecessarily, merely so that they can get to frame their next subject.

10.2   Find locations from which the cameras can use all of their lenses without moving.

The 50mm lens on the camera in *Figure 10/5* takes in all three persons. The 90mm gets either B and C or A and B. The 135mm gets a closeup of either B or C. The 8½″ can frame a small object displayed by any of them.

Fig. 10/5

50 mm   **90mm**   **135mm**   **8 ½″**

10.3   Several playing areas can sometimes be arced around central camera locations.

The floor plan in *Figure 10/6* shows that five areas can be covered without either camera moving except to make minor framing adjustments. Of these areas, A and E need be covered by only one camera; B, C, and D require two cameras. The furniture in each area has been so angled that the performers using it will be facing camera as much as possible when they are addressing their normal centers of attention. In area B, for example,

Fig. 10/6

camera 2 favors the performer in the left chair behind the desk, and camera 1 the performer in the right chair. In area C, camera 1 would favor the standing performer; camera 2 would be perpendicular to the map for unforeshortened closeups of it. In area D, camera 2 would take the persons on the sofa while camera 1 covered the person in the armchair.

11 Compress your settings.

Don't disperse the playing areas of your setting so widely that to cover them requires unnecessary camera placements or needlessly long pans from one subject to another.

For example, the instructor in a program on music appreciation plays a short passage on a phonograph record, then crosses to a chalkboard to diagram the musical construction of the passage. As staged by a student of directing who was used to settings which fill the whole proscenium opening of a theatre, the action went like this (*Figure 10/7*):

Performer plays
record here . . . . then crosses to chalkboard here:

Fig. 10/7

requiring cameras
to move from here . . . . to here.

This caused a needless spread of studio area to be occupied and lighted. It put the cameramen to unnecessary work. Most important, it damaged the pace of the program. Because he had to wait for the cameras to make the transition, the instructor could not proceed immediately from playing the music to diagramming it. Instead, he had to fill in with some needless remarks, verbally vamping until ready, so to speak, with a consequent weakening of his hold on his audience.

There was no need for so diffuse a setting, for unlike the theatre, there was no proscenium frame to fill; nor did the chalkboard have to be so far away to avoid intruding on the action with the record player. The scene in television is only what one sees within the camera frame at any given moment. Pan or tilt the camera a few degrees to what lies just outside the present frame, and you have a totally new background—or, for that matter, simply rearrange the performers within your present frame and you have a very different looking picture.

If, as in *Figure 10/8,* the chalkboard is placed quite close to the record player, a tilt-up of both cameras as the instructor rises will effect a complete change of scene without risking the delay and chance for error that can result from trucking the cameras into new locations.

Fig. 10/8

12   Give moving cameras an orderly path.

When your cameras need to move to one subject after another, arrange the subjects so that the cameras can progress in logical and orderly paths.

Figure 10/9 shows an exhibit of paintings so arranged that, as the two commentators walk from one painting to the next, the cameras drop back in straight paths. As the discussion of each painting nears its end, camera 2 is released from a closeup of the painting to retire to its next location. Camera 1 shows the commentators advancing to the next painting, dollying back in pace with them. Since the cameras repeat this maneuver for every painting, there is little chance for anyone, cameramen or performers, to get confused.

Fig. 10/9

An orderly path should be provided for panning as well as for dollying. *Figure 10/10* represents a tier of shelves containing items to be viewed in closeup, one after another, as each is discussed. Numerals indicate the order in which the items should be discussed so that the camera can follow the smooth and even progression traced by the arrowed dash line. Note that item #4 comes directly beneath item #3 so that

Fig. 10/10

the camera can tilt down to it directly rather than having to retrace awkwardly to the left end of the shelf, thus breaking the rhythm of the progression and risking a possible delay in keeping up with the discussion.

13   Minimize lens changes.

Particularly on unrehearsed and unscripted programs, the time taken to change and focus a lens may be enough to miss a shot. To guard against this:

13.1   Advise your performers to give sufficient time for lens changes.

For example, on a two-camera program you have used camera 1 on a wide lens to establish a performer with a number of variously sized objects which he is to discuss. He begins with a large object, which you take in a closeup by camera 2. He will need to talk about this large object long enough so that camera 1 can change to a narrow lens for the closeup of a much smaller object to which he will refer next.

In *Figure 10/11,* A, followed by camera 2, has just approached the counter to introduce the viewers to B, who will presently show A the label on a jug. Camera 1 is in the only good position to take a closeup of this label. First, however, it is needed for a one-shot of B, which will provide a better notion of B's appearance than the introductory view of his profile in the two-shot by camera 2. The lens which camera 1

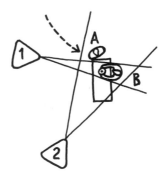

Fig. 10/11

will use for the one-shot of B is too wide for a sufficiently close shot of the label. Instead of tilting camera 1 down from face to label, therefore, the director must return to camera 2's two-shot, freeing camera 1 to change to a narrower lens. Only after this change can B refer to the label. The director must caution him against showing the label as soon as A approaches him.

13.2   Fewer lens changes are needed if, when a series of closeups is to be taken, the subjects can be grouped in relatively uniform sizes.

When a performer has a series of variously sized objects to show in closeup, it may be possible for him to regulate the order in which he refers to them. Rather than showing first a big object, then a small one, then a middle-sized one, then a big one, and so on, he may be able to show all the big ones, then all the middle-sized ones, then all the small ones.

This principle also applies to a series of pictures stacked on an easel. Ideally, such pictures should be uniformly sized so that no lens changes at all are required. If the pictures you have procured are not uniform, it may pay to have them re-photographed to identical dimensions.

14   Locate and maneuver your subjects with regard for camera location and the lens being used.

Besides moving your camera in relation to the subjects, remember that you can also move the subjects in relation to the camera, arranging them to suit the location of the camera and the lens it is using, thus eliminating needless lens changes and camera redeployment. This can be done by applying a principle which has already been introduced to you:

14.1   Place small subjects closer to the lens, big ones farther from it.

Here are some further applications of the principle:

Example 1: Figure 10/12 diagrams the opening of an interview program. Camera 1 is assigned to the opening titles and, quickly thereafter, a closeup of B as he is introduced by A. To hasten 1's time between these shots, the director has first determined what lens will be needed for the closeup of B, then located the titles at a distance which will allow

Fig. 10/12

them to be taken by the same lens. Notice also that, in order to minimize panning time, the titles are only a few degrees off 1's angle towards B rather than, for instance, at the place indicated by the dash lines.

Example 2: The principle also applies to the deployment of characters in dramatic action. Consider a sequence in which A, entering his front hall from outdoors, notices an unfamiliar hat on the hall rack and looks surprised. At the door of the living room he meets his wife, B, who tells him that they have a visitor. She takes him into the room and introduces him to the visitor, C.

Figure 10/13 shows how this sequence has been arranged for a continuous pan by a stationary camera. The hatrack is just far enough from camera 2 so that the upper part of A and the part of the rack which holds the unfamiliar hat will fill the screen when A has reached the rack. After this, A comes even closer to camera, where his surprised expression will be especially evident. Turning to enter the living room, he moves just far

Fig. 10/13

enough away from camera to allow room for B to enter the shot. The introduction to C is staged still farther from camera, where all three characters can be framed.

The principle demonstrated here is especially recommended for productions done on one camera. For changes of framing in such productions, the only alternative is to dolly or zoom in and out, which, if done frequently and hurriedly, will make the viewer conscious of camera movement and perhaps unduly restless as well.

Even when multiple cameras are available, it may be desirable, as in the just cited instance of A and his visitor, to sustain a sequence on one camera. The avoidance of takes to other cameras preserves the continuity of A's approach to his guest. And since takes can lose their effectiveness through needless repetition, the sustained shot also protects the impact of the next shot, which will be taken by camera 1 of the guest when he announces the purpose of his visit.

15   Let your actors do the walking—more than the cameramen.

Unrehearsed lens changes and camera redeployment are liable to result in late shots, missed shots, or poor shots. For productions which involve a large number and variety of shots (as dramas, for instance, often do), it is sometimes more feasible and less expensive to devote more time to dry rehearsals with the performers outside of the studio than to facilities rehearsals with the cameramen. If so, it makes sense to keep the camerawork as simple as possible, putting more obligation on the performers to be at the right distances and facing in the right directions to get the shots you need. The ultimate is attained when all that the cameramen have to do is stay put and focus what unfolds before their never-changing lenses!

Chapter 11

Concealing Mechanics

1 Don't distract your viewer's attention from the content to the technique by which the content is communicated.

Be proficient at "the art that conceals art."

1.1 This instruction does not apply if the audience accepts a device as a necessary and acknowledged part of the communication.

Students watching a televised biology lesson are likely to realize the advantage of having a television camera connected to the microscope and, seeing it thus on the screen, will subordinate their consciousness of it as an instrument to their interest in what it has to show. And if an audience has been made aware from the outset that it is watching a frankly "studio" type of program, it is not likely to resent the sight of microphones in the picture or object to a performer asking that the camera move in for a closer look at something. In a program which aims to create the illusion of action existing quite independently of television, of course, the intrusion of the tools of television would be quite out of place.

In any kind of production, however, there are other ways to distract the viewer besides showing him the tools of the trade. For example:

2 Avoid taking new shots without a reason that is evident to the viewer.

You can distract and perplex the viewer by taking a new shot without a reason that is evident to him. Although you may have your own technical reasons for getting off a camera (it's burning in, perhaps, or must be released to set up for a subsequent shot), all the viewer sees is that the subject has jumped unaccountably in size or screen location without providing any more significant visual information than he had before. So there is punctuation. Where there shouldn't be, like inserting. A period in the middle of a sentence.

2.1   The most valid reason for taking a new shot is to tell what the previous shot could not have told, or told as well.

Therefore, one changes cameras to reveal a newly significant subject or to eliminate one no longer significant—or, remaining with the same subject, to show a newly significant aspect of it, either by changing the angle of view or by altering the amount of area framed as the action expands or contracts.

2.2   Think twice about changing shots merely for visual variety.

A reason sometime advanced for changing shots is to avoid monotony when the subject (a public speaker, for instance) must remain on the screen as the sole center of interest for minutes at a time. Hence, usually at quite arbitrary moments, the director takes a different view of the subject which rarely reveals anything new and meaningful concerning the program content that did not appear in the previous shot.

It would appear that such a shot change provides only a superficial and not very lasting regeneration of interest. Interest would seem to come, rather, from perceiving whatever new, significant information the new shot reveals. Therefore, if constant visual interest is held to be desirable, the main problem, seemingly, is to select and develop a topic that is visually expressive. And if shot changes are wanted, the first step in making them possible is to introduce changes in the subject matter which will motivate the shot changes.

If this cannot be done, if the presentation depends mainly on speech by a single performer, one should try for a visually expressive speaker. To the extent that his features and gestures and bodily attitudes are varied and meaningful there will be less need for an arbitrary change of shot.

2.3   Sometimes frequent shot changes are not appreciated.

Although a young director may not believe it, some audiences are capable of becoming quite engrossed in what a speaker has to say to them and of being satisfied with what visual expression they can read in his face, hands and bodily attitude; and once in visual communion with the speaker's eyes, they can be irritated to have this contact and their mental concentration broken by an unmotivated change in their relationship to him. A change of visual stimulus which calls for interpretation by their visual channel can disturb their reception through the aural channel and therefore may damage their assimilation of auditory subject matter such as intellectual discourse, poetry or music.

2.4   Really pay attention to the program content.

Some directors, it seems, call for new shots simply because they get restless sitting in the control room without enough to do. Their job is to call the shots, and call them they will. They are more interested in shot calling than in the nature of the program content. They do not really listen to the content or try to identify themselves with the target audience.

But you should. Then, if in your best judgment new takes are indicated, try not to make them arbitrary. By placing them between the paragraphs of a speech or the phrases of music, you can use them to clarify the structure of the communication. New shots can reinforce major changes in the development of the subject matter; and when the new shots are also closer ones, they can emphasize the arrival of a more important or more exciting part of the proceedings.

2.5   You should be able to advance a reason for every shot you take.

The reason should not derive from your own requirements, but from the content and purpose of the communication. This is the only kind of reason which will be understood by the audience and which will therefore keep the audience immersed in the program content.

3   Avoid camera movement without a reason which is evident to the viewer.

Evident reason should exist not only for takes, but also for every other kind of picture change, including those produced by camera movement such as by panning and dollying.

3.1   Provide a lead for the camera to follow.

When a camera pans to follow a moving subject, the motivation is evident—but to see the picture suddenly move off a stationary subject without knowing why may startle the viewer, puzzle him, and make him think, "The camera is moving," whereas he should be concentrating solely on the new pictorial information which the camera is bringing into view.

This distraction can be prevented by providing a lead for the camera to follow. The lead can be visual, as when a performer glances towards a new center of interest before the camera pans to it, or as when a demonstrator gestures along a row of items which the camera is to traverse. The lead can also be auditory, as when a voice or noise is heard outside the frame, or a speaker within the frame directs attention to something which is out of sight. Both auditory and visual leads are supplied by the panelist who, during introductions, turns towards his neighbor, saying, "And on my left . . ." to motivate the pan.

3.2   If a camera movement continues after the reason for it has ceased, attention will go from the subject matter to the mechanics of the movement.

For example, two performers walk forward to investigate something in the foreground, the camera dollying back as they advance. All will be well if the camera keeps pace with them so that when they stop, it stops—but if, through some need to adjust its framing, it continues to dolly back, its movement will become noticed. The purpose of the movement was to accompany the performers to their destination. Once they have reached that destination, any further camera motion will impinge on the viewer's consciousness as an unmotivated mechanical adjustment.

3.3   Suit the pace of the camera movement to the viewer's urgency to see what it reveals.

Sometimes a camera movement may call attention to itself because its pace is inconsistent with the degree of motivation for a change of picture. A gunshot may be fired outside the frame, motivating the camera to pan rapidly towards the source of the explosion. This movement (called a whip pan or swish pan) occurs so suddenly that it will be disturbing if not justified by the urgency of the situation. One does not use it to pan to someone who says, "I think I'd like a second lump of sugar if you don't mind, old fellow."

Another kind of swift picture change can be achieved by the zoom-in. Thus, one may zoom in rapidly on a ringing telephone which is expected to carry a message from the governor concerning the reprieve of a condemned man. Since the matter is urgent, the speed of the zoom is justified.

Sometimes, however, a camera movement can exceed the speed limit. For example, a director may have a vocalist in long shot and wish to dolly in on her to support the climax of her rendition. This is a fairly subtle motivation, which will not strike the viewer as an urgent reason for moving closer; hence his concentration may be disturbed unless the camera creeps in ever so gradually.

Too slow can be as disturbing as too fast. The director is supposed to show his viewers what they want to see when they want to see it. It will not do to be late in panning to the product which the demonstrator has started to extol, or to delay the dolly-back when the master of ceremonies says, "Standing beside me is a young lady I think you are going to appreciate." Tardiness of even a second is sometimes enough to blur the desired accent. The very moment your viewers perceive the need for a change, you must be ready to deliver it.

3.4   If you must make a technical adjustment, make it as impercepti-ble as possible.

Sometimes you must move the camera for some technical reason which is not evident to the audience. Thus, when the shot is of long dura-tion and the camera tube is "sticky," a pan or dolly may be required to prevent the image from burning in. If so, make the best of a bad bargain by keeping the movement as imperceptible as possible. Apply similar caution to compositional adjustments, as when the headroom is wrong or a studio card has been poorly framed and the camera must move to set things right.

4   Avoid obviously repetitive devices.

4.1   Techniques are liable to show when they are repeated in too frequent and obvious a rhythm.

The wrong way to shoot a tennis match is to station a camera off one end of the net and wag it back and forth as the ball changes courts.

A poor way to take a series of close shots is to zoom in and out, in and out, in and out. If you are confined to one camera with zoom lens for a sequence which requires a number of closeups, remember the advice in the preceding chapter about placing subjects for one-camera sequences.

4.2   Consciousness of camerawork can result from a monotonous rep-etition of the same shot sequence.

Thus, avoid a pattern of: two-shot, closeup, two-shot, closeup, two-shot, closeup—or: closeup host, closeup guest, closeup host, closeup guest *ad infinitum.* A repetitive series of one-shots can be varied by an occasional group shot. A static situation with limited opportunities for shot variety can sometimes be improved by providing some reason and opportunity for the performers to move into different physical relationships.

The more frequently you cut from camera to camera at the opening of a sequence involving subjects in fixed positions, the more quickly you can exhaust your possible number of shot combinations. These may then have to be repeated over and over, each time becoming more apparent and monotonous.

5   Restrict technical virtuosity to the proper times and places.

There comes a time in the development of some directors when they tire of conventional methods and want to express their virtuosity. This may lead them to overuse the effects amplifier, replacing simple takes with fancy wipes—or to use wide-angle lenses and unusual camera angles to produce extremely foreshortened perspective—or to shoot from inside the fireplace, or from outside the window, or through the banister railing, or between straddled legs, or from some other vantage point where it is difficult to imagine an observer being located. Since such shots are usually out of harmony with those which have preceded them, they call attention to themselves as exploitations of technique rather than as sincere and modest servants of the communication purpose. Unless the show is consistently stylized to allow such *tours de force,* they are as inappropriate as the setting for an illusionistic play which wins applause as the curtain opens.

6   Take some responsibility on yourself for inept operation by your crews.

It is obviously unfortunate when the wrong slide comes up, or cameras lurch and waver, go out of frame or focus, or are late getting their shots. Such ineptitudes not only call attention to the mechanics of production, but to faulty mechanics as well.

Although you may wish to pass the blame for such short-comings to inexperienced crews or insufficient rehearsal time, be sure that you yourself have not failed to give sufficiently clear instructions, to allow enough time for lens changes and camera repositioning, or to have the camera on a lens which can be kept in focus while dollying. If facilities rehearsal is short, have you accomplished everything you should prior to it? Have you made the most efficient use of that rehearsal? (In this connection, you may wish to read the chapter on "Efficiency" in Part Two of this book.)

7   Look and listen critically, and insist on as much perfection as it is possible to achieve under the circumstances.

There is much truth in the observation that professionalism is, in the main, a painstaking attention to details. An example of attention to details is provided by the following note, written to a student director about a single camera movement in one of his studio exercises:

"You ask a pedestal camera to make a fast dolly-in towards a standing performer. First, be sure that the cameraman is using a wide lens which will make focusing easier for him and give him the shortest possible distance to traverse with his dolly. Note that, even so, he goes slightly out of focus. Find the trouble: he doesn't keep his hand on the focus knob. Get him to practice and memorize how much he has to turn the knob, and with what acceleration as he comes closer to the subject. Next, notice that as he comes closer, he has to tilt up more and more, changing the angle of view for no apparent reason. Therefore, better have him pedestal up to put the camera lens at the subject's eye level. Then see how the camera wavers during the move. To simplify the operator's control of it, have him lock every moving part he doesn't need: pan, tilt and boom height. Now, observe that he comes so close to the subject that facial distortion is apparent. Hence, give him a framing where you want him to stop. Lastly, recognize that the dolly-in lags a little behind the action, so work to improve its timing."

All this for a single camera movement! True, it involved an inexperienced operator; but owing to job turnover, cameramen at local stations are not always experienced, and even those who can handle the mechanical aspects of the operation may need to have their esthetic standards raised. And no matter how professional the crew, there are always details to work on. It's possible to work more than an hour on a single one-minute commercial without attaining a perfection to be really proud of.

8   Don't bite off more than you can chew.

Much of the smoothness of your production may depend on how elaborate an undertaking you attempt. Laudable as their courage and optimism may be, student directors often attempt lighting and staging effects which are too ambitious to perfect with the time and resources available. Take the conditions into account—the competences of your production crew members, how much teamwork they are capable of achieving, the amount of studio space available, the capacities of the equipment, the possible existence of other projects which will interfere with yours—and if these conditions seem unfavorable for achieving what you have conceived, either seek to improve the conditions before your time in studio, or modify your conception to what you can reasonably hope to achieve under the circumstances. A dry-ice cloud effect isn't worth it if, to make it work properly, you have to neglect more essential aspects of your production.

Chapter 12

Spatial Relationships

1   Don't perplex your viewer by failing to show him how each new picture is related to the preceding ones. It looks like rain.

The second sentence above was out of context. You couldn't relate it to what you'd been reading previously. It probably startled you and puzzled you, interrupting your train of thought. The same thing can happen to your viewer if you show him a picture which he cannot immediately relate to the program context. True, your picture may not be as obviously unrelated as the sentence was to its context. Nevertheless, as this and the two following chapters will reveal, there are several ways in which new shots may fail to connect smoothly enough with the shots which have preceded them. This chapter is concerned with spatial connections.

2   The viewer must know where things are located in relation to one another.

He will know this quite certainly as long as you remain on one camera. Even when it pans and dollies, the camera traces a connecting path from one subject to another. Space in this instance is continuous. But by taking a new shot, you chop space apart. To use a term synonymous in the trade with "take," you *cut*. You cut to a new location or a new subject; or if you remain with the same subject, you cut to a different portion of it, or a different side of it, or a new relation between it and its environment—but when cutting these pieces, you must assemble them in an intelligible patern.

When shooting, then, take pains to clarify the location of people and things and the physical relationships between them.

3   Show where new subjects are located with reference to those previously seen.

For example, what is wrong with the following shot series?

An interviewer, shown alone, introduces his guest.
The guest, alone.
The interviewer again, still alone.
The guest again, still alone.

The error is that the two persons are never seen together. The viewer never learns whether they are side by side or across the room from each other.

3.1   Clarify the position not only of persons but also of things:

Chest shot of a scientist (seated at a counter which is not shown).
Pan with him as he rises, moves a few steps, and stops.
Closeup of a microscope and, presently, a hand adjusting it.

Where is the microscope? Whose is the hand? Actually, the microscope is farther down the same counter at which the scientist was sitting, and the hand is his hand—but from the pictures who would know it?

3.2   Clarification may also be needed when the shots are confined to the body of one person.

Consider these shots of a golf professional, who is demonstrating how to putt:

The "pro," from waist up, talking to camera.
A body, from waist down, with hands holding a golf club.

Do the two parts of the body belong to the same person? One cannot be certain from this pictorial dissection.

4   Connect up space by panning, tilting, or dollying back.

To clarify relationships such as those in the example just cited, one solution is to pan, tilt, or dolly back, depending on which of these camera movements is appropriate. In shooting the golf "pro," the director could have tilted down from the upper to the lower part of his body. In the case of the interviewer and his guest, the director could have panned from the interviewer to the guest—or he could have dollied back from the interviewer into a two-shot which included the guest. In all cases, the camera would traverse a continuous path to connect one subject with another.

5   Introduce the subject of the next shot in the present shot.

This is another way to correct the examples: you introduce the subject of the next shot in the present shot. Before taking a one-shot of the guest, you take a two-shot which shows him with the interviewer. Before taking the shot of the "pro's" hands and club, you show his whole body. In the case of the scientist and his microscope, you have him rise in a shot which includes both him and the counter top. When you pan with him, using this framing, the microscope will slide into view as he nears it, and its relation to him will be evident before it is isolated in a closeup.

6   Use an establishing shot.

Each of the wider shots just recommended is an example of an establishing shot—so called because it establishes the location of a detail with reference to the total situation of which it is a part.

6.1   Although, in the examples just cited, it precedes the closer shot, it need not always do so, provided it occurs in time to forestall perplexity.

For example, it might be possible to take one-shots both of the interviewer and of his guest before taking a third shot which included them together. It is unlikely that the viewer would have worried about their spatial relationship until then.

6.2   An establishing shot is advisable at or near the beginning of any sequence involving several components which are in the same location.

It establishes the overall relationships so that the viewer will remain oriented when, in the shots that follow, he sees the components separately or in various partial combinations. Thus, an overall shot of a dining table will prepare the way for various closer shots of the diners who are seated at it.

6.3   When the location is too wide to be easily discerned in a stationary shot, the establishing may be done with a pan.

For example, if you are shooting at the location of a wrecked train, an opening pan along the cars will prepare for a series of subsequent shots, each focusing on a different detail of the disaster.

7   Establish whatever the viewer will be bothered by not seeing.

Apart from establishing relationships with reference to subsequent shots, you need to shoot wide enough to establish what is happening in the present shot. For example, a performer who has been shown from waist up suddenly sinks down in the frame to chest level. Then his hand rises into the frame with a glass from which he drinks. Why did he sink? He was sitting down on a stool, which the director failed to show. Where did the glass come from? It was on a table, which the director also failed to show.

8   Sometimes you will need to re-establish.

8.1   Do this to remind viewers of the overall relationship.

After a fairly long series of shots which are restricted to parts of a situation, a reminding view of the ensemble will not only provide shot variety, but will also renew a sense of unity between the components.

8.2   Do this to reveal changed relationships which result from subjects moving to new locations during a scene.

It is often advisable to show these changes as they occur. Consider, for example, the following shot series:

A and B (both standing) and C (in chair).
Several shots of only A and B.
Shot including C (at piano).

What? C at the piano—how did he get over there? The director knows, and probably looked through the control room window and saw him move. But the viewer at home knows nothing except what he sees on the screen.

9   Use something in common to link shots of separate components.

When two components of a scene are taken in separate shots, one way to clarify their physical relationship is to keep something common to the shots of each. Thus, the slanting top of a grand piano may form a mutual point of reference for relating separate shots of a singer and his accompanist. Or the mutual referent may be a person who, having appeared in the first shot, remains in view in the second.

Chapter 13

Consistency

Again you are asked to remember:

1   Don't perplex your viewer by failing to show him how each new picture is related to the preceding ones.

One way to promote the relationship between shots of the same situation is to be consistent in your pictorial treatment of them. In what follows you will learn how to do. this—or, in a sense, how not to do it, for you will be reading about several types of *in*consistency which the director should avoid.

2   Avoid inconsistent backgrounds.

A conversing couple is taken in reverse angle shots which reveal alternately different backgrounds—one of drapes, perhaps, and the other of bricks in a fireplace wall; or one sharply focused and the other blurred; or one light in tone and the other dark; or (in color television) one red, perhaps, and the other green. In any of these instances the conversation almost seems to be taking place in two different locations.

The discrepancy may not be bothersome if, by virtue of establishing shots, the audience has had a chance to view the overall setting and notice the variations in it. Otherwise, depending on the nature of the discrepancy, you may have to locate the performers against a more consistent background, or change the camera angles, or balance the background illumination, or match more closely the focal lengths of the lenses you are using on each camera.

3   Avoid inconsistent illumination.

When the light comes principally from one direction, but the cameras aim from widely divergent directions, the same subject may look flat and bright in one shot and dark or contrasty in another. The audience may accept this difference if it is aware of the light source and realizes that it is directional in character. Otherwise, the illumination for the two shots should be matched more evenly.

4   Avoid inconsistent variations in the light levels fed into camera chains.

On this subject review what was stated in Chapter 4 concerning undesirable fluctuations in scene brightness and in the density of projected materials.

5   Avoid inconsistency from shot to shot in the location of subjects on the screen.

5.1   When two subjects of similar screen size are taken in alternating shots, their headroom should be similar.

Otherwise, there will be a bobbing up and down effect as the shots succeed one another.

5.2   Prevent jump cuts.

A single subject will seem to jump suddenly from one screen location to another on a take between cameras which are framing the subject at similar scale, but not in identical parts of their fields. Suppose, for instance, that a punted football is picked up by a second camera when it is getting out of range of the first. If the ball is moving towards the right, say, and the second camera frames it more to the left than did the first camera, it will seem to jump backwards on the take. A jump can also occur in a sequence taken by a single camera if this has been recorded on film or video tape and a short section of the action has been removed. An effect similar to a jump cut will appear when the subjects of successive shots are so similar that one expects them to be consistently aligned, yet they are not. Thus, the lettering on sequential captions may seem to jump back and forth or up and down as the captions replace one another, unless the lettering has been laid out and framed uniformly.

5.3   Make it easy for your viewers to follow a subject from one shot to the next without having to hunt for it in a new part of the screen.

Example: A performer is conversing with a person on either side of him. Instead of establishing all three together, the director takes successive two-shots, first of the performer with the person on his left, then of the performer with the person on his right. On the take between these shots, the performer will jump from one side of the screen to the other.

5.4   Maintain the relative screen locations of two subjects when taking them both together in successive shots.

Two performers, A and B, are facing each other. Camera 1 takes a two-shot towards A over B's left shoulder. Then camera 2 also takes a two-shot towards A, but over B's right shoulder. On the take the relative positions of the two will be reversed. This is illustrated by the left diagram in *Figure 13/1*. To correct the trouble, imagine a line running between the two persons and, as in the right diagram, keep both of your cameras on one side of this line.

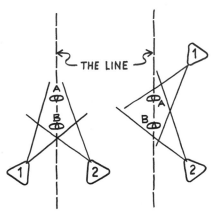

Fig. 13/1

6   Avoid inconsistency regarding the direction in which subjects face and move.

6.1   Again, keep your cameras on the same side of the line.

If you shoot as in *Figure 13/2*, although your performers are actually facing
each other, they will face in the same direction on the screen.

Assigned to shoot the stock car races
at State Fair Park, you place one camera inside the track to get shots of the grandstand
and the other camera outside the track.
When the races begin, you will find that, on
each take, the cars reverse direction on the
screen. In this case, the track corresponds to
the imaginary line, and you have failed to
keep your cameras on the same side of it.

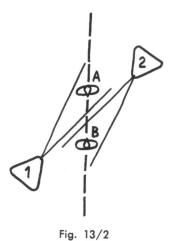

Fig. 13/2

*6.2   If you shoot towards opposite sides from a moving vehicle, the
scene will stream by in opposite directions.*

The shots which fail to match for this reason may be reconciled by
separating them with another shot, headed in the direction the vehicle is
moving.

*6.3   When two persons are facing each other in conversation, suc-
cessive profiles of each taken separately should still appear to be facing
each other.*

Fig. 13/3

In the framed shots of *Figure 13/3,* this is not the case. Although A's head is actually on the left of B's, it appears in the one-shot on the right side of the frame—and the same in reverse is true of B's head. Even in column I of *Figure 13/4,* where each head is centered, it is not as evident that the two persons are talking to each other as it is in column II, where the heads are off-centered sufficiently to correspond to their actual relationship.

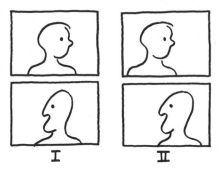

Fig. 13/4

7   Avoid inconsistent camera angles.

Unless new information is revealed by changing the point of view, it can be confusing to observe the same subject in succeeding shots from different angles.

If a speaker who is addressing the camera is taken successively in shots from widely divergent directions, his audience contact is broken, requiring him for no evident reason to shift his gaze towards the second camera. Meanwhile, the viewer, having to identify himself unexpectedly with a new point of view, may feel as if he has been forcibly and unaccountably transplanted from one seat to another.

It is also disturbing when a performer, saying, "Look at this photograph," is shown holding the photograph at a pronounced angle to the observer so that a closeup of it can be taken by another camera which is some distance apart from the present one. To avoid this disturbance, both cameras should shoot as nearly as possible from the same direction.

In a program on how to play chess, the chessboard is viewed first from the side; then, as one of the players moves a piece, a new shot is taken over this player's shoulder. This obliges the viewer to re-orient himself to the disposition of pieces on the board, which has probably already been difficult enough for him to apprehend.

7.1   *Consistency should apply also to vertical angles.*

In shooting a seated couple, a director uses one camera on a pedestal mount, which has been lowered to take a two-shot from very nearly the couple's eye level. For a closeup of one of the couple, however, he must use a tripod-mounted camera with its lens fixed at a height suitable for taking standing persons. To use this camera close to a seated subject will oblige it to angle down quite steeply in contrast to the pedestal camera's more level angle. This inconsistency can be avoided by changing to a longer lens on the tripod camera and pulling the camera back to where its declination will be more gradual.

When there is a motivation for a change of vertical angle, of course, the sense of inconsistency will not exist. In televising a square dance, takes may seem quite logical between a camera on the studio floor to provide a normal view and a camera shooting from a gallery to show off the movement patterns of the dancers—but at intermission, when the master of ceremonies interviews the square dance caller, takes between the normal angle and the high angle will seem inexplicable and inappropriate.

7.2 Action can become confusing when it is shown from too great a variety of arbitrary angles.

The safest way to keep the audience oriented is to stick to a consistent pattern of shooting angles, avoiding the unique shot which is suddenly taken from some altogether unexpected direction (unless there is clear motivation for it). For example, having taken all of your previous shots from inside the room, don't insert a single shot from outside the window simply because you fancy it as unusual or think that it is easier to do this than to get the subject of your shot to face one of the other cameras.

The unity of an action should be reinforced by consistency of camera treatment. If a line of panelists are all looking towards the master of ceremonies who is stationed off one end of their row, it can be quite confusing, when separate shots of them are taken, to see some of them in profile and others full face. Their parallel action could be communicated better by choosing camera angles which will keep them all facing the same way on the screen. To borrow advice from a book on literary style, "one should express coordinate ideas in similar form."

8 Avoid inconsistencies of screen size.

The principle of expressing coordinate ideas in similar form should also regulate the scale of subjects on the screen. When one member of a scene expresses something of greater significance or intensity than what has come before, there is reason to reinforce this expression with a closer shot. On the other hand, there are many scenes wherein the participants make more or less equal contributions. In a sequence during which an interviewer asks the same question of three guests in turn, it would not make sense to see one guest in a chest shot, the next in a waist shot, and the third in a tight closeup. Since their functions and the weight of their remarks are coordinate, their screen scale should be likewise.

9   Avoid the inconsistency of switching between a moving and a stationary camera on the same subject.

Example: When a camera pans or trucks with a person who is moving across the scene, the person maintains a fixed position on the screen while all the stationary objects within view stream across the frame. If a switch is then made to a motionless camera, the objects halt abruptly and the person starts to move across the frame. This can be a quite noticeable and inexplicable reversal.

Example: A vocalist is singing the last measures of his selection while a camera, to support the climax, is dollying in on him from a long shot. The camera reaches his knees and is still dollying when the director takes a stationary shoulder shot. The effect of this take on a viewer is something like being catapulted forward from a moving vehicle which has suddenly stopped.

10   Avoid inconsistencies in treatment between various parts of the production.

Example: Dynamic opening titles accompanied by an exciting or grandiose musical theme introduce a mathematics lesson on quadratic equations.

11   When shooting in segments, avoid inconsistences between one segment and another related segment.

This problem is ever present when shooting film, for action in film production is rarely continuous for long periods. Some film cameras have to be stopped frequently for rewinding or reloading. Even when the film magazine is large and the camera motor driven, a pause after every shot may be desirable for changing the camera position, lights, lenses or other production elements. Shots may be taken over a range of weeks, at different locations, with differing conditions of light and weather, and in a sequence far different from that in which they are eventually assembled. It is possible to record two shots from the same sequence at widely separated times—yet they must correspond in lighting, audio quality, grain and contrast characteristics of the film stock, exposure, position of properties in the setting, appearance of the performers' hair and attire, and still other details.

11.1   One way to achieve this correspondence is to keep accurate records of all factors which must be duplicated.

These factors include the physical position of all objects in the scene, the position and dimmer settings of lighting instruments, the f-stops and distance settings of camera lenses, and the type of film stock used. Polaroid still photographs may provide useful visual records of the scene to be matched.

11.2   When a performance has been halted between shots, there is often a problem of matching action.

To make the action seem continuous, the performers' physical attitudes must appear the same at the beginning of the new shot as at the end of the previous one. One solution is to take the new shot from a different angle in order to prevent a direct comparison. Another solution is to cut during an action so pronounced that it will impel the audience's attention across the break and distract it from noticing possible discrepancies in the static elements of the two shots. It is more difficult to detect mismatches when the subjects move than when they sit still for comparison.

When filming such a transition, it is advisable to record the complete action twice (both at the end of the first shot and at the beginning of the second), not only so that the performers can deliver the necessary flow and follow-through, but also that the film editor can cut wherever he finds the smoothest match between the two versions.

Chapter 14

Extreme or Abrupt
Shot Changes

1   A change of shot content should not be so extreme or abrupt that it startles or puzzles (unless these reactions are intentional).

This chapter discusses ways to avoid these reactions when they are not intentional, thus helping to maintain the viewer's immersion in the program content.

2   Avoid extreme changes of scale in successive shots of the same subject unless there is adequate motivation for them.

Example: A full shot of a person is followed by a tight closeup of him. This would be adequately motivated had the person just been singled out, for instance, as guilty of some crime. The announcement of his guilt would throw attention strongly on him, particularly on his face, where his reaction would likely be most evident. Under less dramatic circumstances, however, the change in screen size is too extreme for the audience to adjust to readily.

2.1   To temper such changes, insert a medium shot between the two extremes.

When a brook is too wide to jump without a taxing effort, one can put a stepping stone half way across it. The medium shot is similar in purpose to the stone. One might also walk across a plank to the stone, then step to land from there. Similarly, one might dolly in to the medium shot, then take the closeup.

3   Unless there is adequate motivation, avoid extreme changes of screen direction in successive shots of the same subject.

Example: A shot showing a moving subject approaching from right to left is followed by one of it approaching from left to right. At the instant of change, the audience can have difficulty appreciating that the same subject is involved in both shots—or, appreciating that, it may be uncertain whether the subject has changed or maintained its course—and if it has maintained its course, what is the reason for viewing it from a reversed direction?

3.1   To temper such changes, insert a transitional view of the subject moving directly towards camera.

As with the change in screen size, this remedy inserts an in-between step in order to accomplish the change by degrees.

4   Special techniques are usually needed when omitting a segment from a course of action involving the same subject or subjects.

Such omissions, common in film editing, allow one to dispense with less significant or less interesting portions of the action, jumping from one high spot to another. The jumps, however, should not seem abrupt and illogical.

Example: After showing a baseball player in the bullpen, you want to show his turn at bat, but wish to dispense with his uneventful walk from the bullpen to home plate. Yet to cut, as his walking commences, to a shot of him already facing the pitcher would make a disturbing jump.

4.1   In such situations you can apply out-of-frame into-frame.

Thus, you let him walk out of the bullpen shot and enter the shot at home plate, From this, the audience will understand that one phase of the action is over and that another is beginning; consequently, it will not worry about the eliminated time.

4.2   For certain other cases of omitted action you can use the cut-away.

You wish to show only the highlights of a baseball game—but how can you jump coherently from a situation in one inning to a different state of affairs in a later inning? You can separate the shots which will not correspond, cutting away from the central action to insert a shot of something on the sidelines, such as the scoreboard or the spectators. By this separation of the mismatched shots you prevent a direct comparison between them.

4.3   Another technique is the cut-in.

With this, instead of departing from the central action, you insert a closeup detail of that action. Thus, suppose that you wish to film the erection of a brick wall without keeping the camera on it, brick by brick, yet juxtaposed takes of the wall at various discrete levels will make it seem to grow by leaps. Therefore, you separate these shots with cut-ins of masons' trowels being wielded and other details of the work.

4.4   To bridge between stages in a process of growth without inserting supplementary details, use the dissolve.

This would apply to the brick wall sequence just cited. If you are not interested in showing the masons' activities, if you would prefer to say in effect, "The wall grew . . . and grew . . . and grew . . . ," you could juxtapose shots of the wall at various levels provided that you joined them, not with takes but with dissolves.

5   The dissolve is useful for accommodating the viewer to a new visual circumstance for which he has not otherwise been prepared.

When a new and unexpected circumstance is introduced by a take, it hits one suddenly and therefore momentarily startles or bewilders. Since it comes immediately after the previous shot, the viewer may try to associate it with what he has just been watching. Thus, when the levels of bricks are joined by takes, he tends to regard them as happening within the same time continuum. In other cases, he is puzzled because the new shot is out of context. If this reaction lasts but an instant it is enough to interrupt the continuity. Some device is needed, therefore, to separate the new context from the old.

In writing, this is commonly accomplished by starting a new paragraph. In television, a related purpose is served by the dissolve. In a dissolve the old picture fades out as the new picture fades in. Since this process normally lasts from two to five seconds or more, it is a separating device, accomplishing in time what the paragraph separation does in space. Also, by reason of the cross-fading, it says in effect, "Look, the present circumstance is phasing out, and a new circumstance is phasing in." Or, in the specific instance of the brick wall, "One period of time is ending, and a new one is beginning." In addition, the dissolve might be called a "get used to it gradually device." Because it develops the new picture by degrees, it allows the viewer to become accommodated to new content which occurs unexpectedly before its relation to the previous context is evident.

By reason of these characteristics, the dissolve is suited to the applications discussed below. In all of these, a new visual subject is being introduced. It is unexpected at the precise time it appears. The audience has not been prepared verbally or by any other means to immediately understand its relation to the present proceedings.

5.1   Dissolve between actions which occur at different periods of time.

Thus, dissolve between the shot of Mac slamming the kitchen door after an argument with his wife and the next shot, which shows him easing his tension at the neighborhood bar.

5.2   Dissolve between actions which occur at different locations.

The example just cited includes a change of place as well as of time. But one also dissolves for a change of place when different characters are involved at the two locations.

5.3   Dissolve between sequences which are presented in different modes.

Thus, dissolve between opening titles and studio action, or between studio action and closing titles.

Dissolve between studio and film sequences—from the news analyst in his armchair to the Arab horsemen galloping across the screen—and vice versa.

5.4   Within a sequence occurring at a single place and time, dissolve to any new subject which, at the instant it appears, is not expected and cannot be immediately connected with the action in progress.

Example: You dissolve from soldiers parading down Main Street to a boy at the curb who is having difficulty with a runny ice cream cone. The audience could hardly have expected this shot. The announcer did not say, "Look at that little boy over there!" No parading soldier could be seen looking off screen and smiling to motivate a take to the source of his amusement. There was no necessary connection between the marching and the boy. Nor did the boy himself take over the action by shouting or crying or doing anything to motivate suddenly cutting from the procession to him.

Example: You have on camera an authority who is explaining advertising media. Having cited the more common media (television, newspapers, magazines, etc.), he remarks, "Besides the mass media, there are a number of what we may call 'collateral media,' or 'secondary media' if you prefer. Among these, as you can see, are calendars of the sort that your local fuel company may mail to you at Christmas time . . ."

At some point in this speech, you are expected to go from the speaker to a series of slides, beginning with one of a calendar, then of a matchbook cover, desk blotter and other examples of the topic. Note that there is no precise cue for this transition. By the time calendars are mentioned, the first slide should already be in view. But before calendars are mentioned, the viewer has not been prepared to understand the relation between them and collateral media. Nor does he expect to see a calendar—or, indeed, any picture change at all. Hence a take to the calendar would puzzle and startle him. So you dissolve.

A like situation maintains throughout the entire slide sequence: the viewer does not know what he will see next or when the change will occur. Therefore, you dissolve from one slide to another. And at the end of the slide sequence, since a return to the speaker is unanticipated at the moment it occurs, you effect it by a dissolve instead of a take.

Getting into the slide sequence would have been different had the speaker, prior to the sequence, pointed to a calendar on the wall of his setting, saying, "Here's an example of what I mean." This prior establishment of the calendar precludes any need to get used to it gradually when the closeup of it appears. To introduce this closeup, therefore, it is proper to use a take.

5.5 A dissolve is sometimes used when it is desired to introduce a new shot without stressing the transition.

A take is an abrupt change. The sudden contrast which it effects between shots is likely to say, "Look, something new and important has happened!" The dissolve is a blend which eases onto the new subject, softening the transition. Hence it is sometimes used for introducing a new shot without stressing the transition.

Example: A subject may remain relatively static for considerable time, providing no motivation for a change of shots; yet a change may seem desirable to combat boredom and allow inspection of the subject from some different, interesting angle. Since there is no important occurrence to be accented, a take to the new picture would arouse false expectations. Therefore, the director softens the transition by using a dissolve.

Sometimes a film editor finds that he has no medium shot with which to bridge between a long shot and a closeup. Therefore, he instructs the laboratory to dissolve between these shots to soften the transition.

There are times when the dissolve does not soften as much as a director would like. These occur when he gets on the wrong camera by mistake or when, for some technical reason, he must release the present camera and substitute another for it on the same subject. Hoping that blending from one camera to the other will disguise the change, he uses a dissolve instead of a take. No doubt this is making the best of a bad bargain, but the best is rarely good enough to prevent some notice of the substitution.

6   Do not use dissolves when they are not required.

6.1   Dissolves to closeups are not required when the subject of the closeup has been visually pointed up in the previous shot and related to the matter at hand.

For example, remember the concluding discussion about the advertising calendar.

6.2   Dissolves are not needed when the subject of the new shot is verbally introduced just before or coincident with the change.

Example: (at the end of opening titles) "Now, for the latest news and views in the world of sports, here's Carl Frank!"

Example: (during a newscast) "We take you now to Philadelphia and Donald Britt."

6.3   Dissolves are not needed to connect a sequence of brief shots which, however varied in time, place or subject, are all evidently serving to develop a pre-established situation, action, or idea.

Example: *foreign planes releasing bombs . . . explosions shattering moored U. S. warships . . . the President addressing Congress . . . civilians being issued uniforms . . . etc.* If not evident from the shots themselves, it will be from the commentary which accompanies them that they are all links in a single chain of action and consequence—the attack on Pearl

Harbor and its aftermath. With this unity apparent to him, the viewer will be prepared to move rapidly from one shot to the next by takes.

Example: *park gate . . . tulip bed . . . kids romping . . . man dozing on bench in sunshine . . . blossoms on tree branch . . . popcorn vendor open for business . . . etc.* As the commentary will clarify, each of these shots is related to the mutual topic, "Spring has come to Lakeside Park."

One may cite virtually every news story on television as an example of this principle. Between news stories, however, or upon returning to the news reporter, it is advisable to dissolve, since then one is introducing the viewer to a new circumstance for which he is not prepared.

7   For an extreme sense of separation between one train of thought or action and another, use the fade-out-and-fade-in.

In this device the first shot fades entirely out before the new shot begins to fade in. If the dissolve is likened to a change between paragraphs, then the fade-out-and-fade-in is like a change between chapters. So much finality, indeed, can be suggested by the complete fading out of picture that it is ordinarily used between programs rather than within them. Within a program, the blank screen following a fade out should last only momentarily lest it slacken overmuch the viewer's current of emotional or intellectual involvement. The dissolve, on the other hand, by overlapping the sections which it connects, always assures the viewer that the program is continuing.

8   For certain special effects (suggested below) transitions may be effected by the wipe.

In a wipe, the new picture progressively displaces the old, sometimes crossing straight-edged from one side to the other, sometimes expanding from one corner as an enlarging rectangle, sometimes growing from the center of the screen in the shape of a circle or diamond, or sometimes opening fanwise though a full 360° angle.

Halted partway, a wipe can split the screen to show actions occurring simultaneously in two places or to present two different aspects of the same subject. By halting the wipe which expands from a corner, one can make space in that corner for a commentator, reserving the rest of the screen for the material about which he is commenting.

8.1   Complete wipes are used as circumstances dictate.

A lateral wipe may follow the exit of persons off one side of the screen as new ones enter from the opposite side to begin a new scene. At the end of a sequence when the subject recedes into the distance at center screen, a contracting wipe such as a closing circle can keep the subject prominent until the last moment. A wipe expanding from center may impart a feeling of growth and development to the beginning of a scene, or induce curiosity by uncovering the subject progressively. In shows of a frankly "theatrical" nature (variety shows, for instance), the wipe may add novelty and decorative style by reason of its dynamic and geometric patterns. For more illusionistic productions, however, it may call attention to itself as a device, thereby disturbing the viewer's immersion in the story.

8.2   Avoid overusing wipes.

When first provided with an amplifier capable of producing wipes, some directors can be so fascinated with the novelty of these effects that they overuse them and fail to consider whether they are using them appropriately.

Chapter 15

Other Visual Transitions

By discussing the dissolve, fade and wipe, the previous chapter opened the subject of visual transitions, which will be continued in this chapter. Whereas the dissolve, fade and wipe are controlled by the television switching panel or, in the case of film, effected in the film laboratory, the transitions to be considered next are produced by moving the camera. They are: the pan, the dolly-in, the dolly-back, the truck, the arc, and (although it involves moving only the lens element within the camera) the zoom.

Most of the common uses of these devices have been listed below.

Uses of the Pan

1   To move the eye progressively from one (usually stationary) subject to another.

Thereby the pan can be used to:

1.1   Establish a connection between the subjects.

By continuously traversing the space between the subjects, the pan establishes a greater connection, both spatial and ideological, between them than were they to be taken in separate shots. Therefore it serves to :

Reinforce such connections as action-consequence, action-reaction and cause-effect. For example, show a closeup of tape running through the heads of a video recorder, then pan up to a monitor which shows the image obtained from this tape.

Associate in a class a number of subjects which share something in common. For example, pan across cans containing various kinds of soup, or across a row of panelists, or from one miner's wife to another as they await news of a mine disaster which mutually affects them.

Inspect the parts of a subject, one after another, without destroying the viewer's awareness of its unity. For example, pan from the bolt and trigger assembly of a rifle to its rear sight to its stacking swivel to its front sight, pausing to identify each in turn.

Preserve the unity of a subject, the details of which would be too small on the screen were they all included in a stationary shot. For example, pan continuously across a landscape, creating a panorama (from which the term "pan" was derived).

Follow an action, preserving its unity, as it is taken up by a succession of different subjects. For example, pan from the first to the second violinist of a string quartet as the lead in a musical passage progresses from one to the other.

Establish various other associations not precisely described above. For example, pan from a crate on the dock to the boat in the distance which is going to take it overseas.

1.2   Follow a lead initiated by one subject which creates interest in a second subject.

Example: a performer looks off screen and the camera moves from him to the object of his attention. A performer points or gestures towards something and the camera moves from him to it.

1.3   Create anticipation when introducing a new subject.

The pan induces a feeling of moving towards something new. Whereas a take shows the new subject completely and immediately, a pan emphasizes the approach towards it, delaying its appearance and revealing it by degrees. Therefore, the pan can be used to:

Build up the importance of a new subject. It does this by delaying, just as a speaker creates emphasis by pausing before an important word or phrase. For example, pan from a master of ceremonies across the inclined

piano cover to the pianist whom he has just introduced. The passage across
the piano cover creates anticipation for the artist one is about to see.

Create suspense, when the camera is panned slowly. Thus used, the
pan can be a movement into the unknown. For example, the camera slowly
traverses the attic of a "haunted" house.

1.4   Concentrate or expand the scope of the subject.

Example: pan from several choir members to the face of the one nearest camera, or from one crate in a warehouse to the pile of crates which is
stored there.

2   To follow a moving subject.

This allows one to:

2.1   Keep the subject sufficiently visible and dominant.

Example: in covering a horse race, a fixed field wide enough to contain the action may make the subjects too small and place them in competition with irrelevant details. Therefore, one closes in on the leading horses
and pans with them.

2.2   Maintain the unity of a movement.

Example: a dance movement, a forward pass, or the cross of an actor
towards a new objective. To cut between cameras, taking successive fields
through which the moving subject passes, might be difficult to do if the
movement is fast, and in any case would make the action jerky and discon-
nected. Cuts would be justified, however, were there multiple stages of the
action to be emphasized, such as (1) aiming an arrow, (2) striking the
target.

2.3   Maintain the unity of a scene which requires a particularly smooth continuity.

When subjects move in such a scene, panning with them will avoid the
necessity for takes, which might introduce unwarranted emphasis or excitement.

2.4   Save takes for occasions when they count.

Indiscriminate use of takes dulls their effectiveness as instruments for
emphasis or excitement. The take which accentuates an important act or

statement will be more effective if it has been preceded by a passage during which no takes are used. A scene in which takes are used frequently to create a sense of activity or excitement will establish its character more successfully if preceded by a scene which has been sustained on one camera.

Uses of the Dolly-in

3   To narrow the field as the area occupied by the significant action contracts.

Example: when one person exits from a three-shot, tighten to frame the two persons remaining. Or, after showing a man raise a glass from the table to his lips, tighten to concentrate on the sip he takes and his reaction to the liquid's taste.

4   To gradually concentrate on the most significant portion of the field.

4.1   After orienting the viewer to the total environment, to narrow his attention to the active elements within it.

This may be useful at the beginning of a scene.

4.2   To increase the impact of an action by progressively closing in on the most expressive portion of it.

Example: move in towards a performer's face, enlarging and clarifying his expression, giving it command of the frame, as when supporting the climax of a solo vocal performance.

5   To follow and maintain at constant scale a subject moving to the rear.

Thus one can:

5.1   Stay with the performer as he moves towards some new objective.

Otherwise he would diminish in the distance, and whatever he is leaving would still remain in the foreground although it is no longer important.

5.2   Increase the force of the performer's move in the consciousness of the viewer.

Example: if the performer is moving aggressively towards an objective, to have the camera move with him at his tempo will empathically move the viewer in with him, thus providing a subjective experience.

6   To identify the viewer subjectively with performers advancing through a terrain.

To shoot through the windshield of a moving car or diving plane gives the viewer an experience similar to that of the performer.

7   To give the viewer a sense of entering an environment.

Example: the camera moves down a street or through a crowd, which streams by on either side of the lens, giving the illusion that one is actually within the locality rather than observing it from a detached position.

8   To alter the relative dominance when two subjects are at different distances from camera.

8.1   To increase the dominance of the foreground figure.

By dollying in with the camera lower than head height, one can increase the size and height of the closer person in relation to that of the farther one.

8.2   To increase the dominance of the background figure.

When the foreground figure is turned to face the more distant one, dollying in to shoot over the foreground figure's shoulder will give more emphasis to the distant figure.

9   To create and then satisfy anticipation.

Example: the camera reveals a new subject at a distance, then moves in closer to investigate it.

Uses of the Dolly-back

10   To include the significant action as its field expands.

Example: the present subjects move farther apart, or new subjects join those already in the shot.

11 To maintain consistent framing of a subject moving forward.

To dolly back with an advancing subject will keep its scale constant instead of letting it enlarge. When the subject is allowed to approach a stationary camera (as when moving into a closeup) more impact may be created than the subject's speech or action justifies.

To dolly back with an advancing subject will keep the same area of the subject constantly in view, whereas if the camera remains stationary, progressive amounts of the subject area will be lost from view.

12 To effect the entrance of new subject matter in the foreground.

12.1 To surprise the audience by revealing that an unsuspected subject is present.

12.2 To give adequate scale to small subjects introduced into the shot.

Example: as a person advances, the camera dollying back with him, his objective is revealed to be a telephone, which enters the frame close to the lens and is therefore large enough on the screen to make an impact consistent with its importance as a new factor in the action.

13 To actively and progressively accumulate new factors in the environment.

Example: as a character advances through a populous environment, the camera dollying back with him, a succession of persons and objects will stream into the picture from each side of the frame and accumulate in the background, making it grow in detail and activity.

14 To expand from a single subject to the context of which it is a part.

14.1 To emphasize the magnitude of the field of action by letting it grow from a small beginning.

Example: start on a close shot of an orchestra conductor and dolly back to reveal the whole orchestra.

14.2 To provoke and progressively satisfy curiosity regarding the total nature of the subject.

Example: start with a close shot of a gun and an outstretched hand on the floor, then draw back to show the body of the victim.

15   To emphasize the expanding significance of an event.

Example: in the example immediately above, continue to draw back as passers by discover the body, detectives arrive, etc.

16   To support a climax which depends on magnitude.

Example: at the close of an instrumental musical number, draw back to reveal the entire orchestra.

17   To create neutral space in which a new subject will presently appear.

Example: the material presently on the screen recedes and (by panning the camera during the dolly-back) moves to one side, leaving an area on the other side into which a new character may enter or over which some printed caption may be superimposed.

18   To identify the viewer subjectively with riders in a moving vehicle.

Example: one shoots backward from the getaway car towards the pursuing police.

19   To signify fiinality by withdrawing from the action.

This lets the subject gradually recede into the distance.

Uses of the Truck

To truck left or right is to move the camera mount sidewise, i.e. in a direction perpendicular to that in which the lens is aiming.

20   To accompany a laterally moving subject, keeping it framed at a constant scale and shown from the same constant angle.

If, instead, one pans with such a subject who is crossing from one side of the scene to the other, the subject will at first enlarge, reaching maximum scale as he passes closest to camera, and then progressively diminish. Also, the angle will reveal progressively less of his front and more of his back. In some instances, this may be exactly what one desires—but if not, one trucks along with the subject.

21   To traverse a long subject, viewing each part of it head on and at a constant scale.

Thus, the camera approximates the view of an officer inspecting a row of soldiers one after another, or of someone walking the length of an assembly line, inspecting each step in the process. With this technique, each element of the subject is given equal value and can be isolated in the frame for complete attention, whereas, were the subject to be panned, elements would become progressively smaller, and more and more of them would appear together in the frame because of their increasing distance from camera.

22   To view a succession of separate subjects from a consistent direction.

The subjects might be artifacts, arranged in a row on a shelf—or they might be pictures, hung side by side on a wall. In the latter instance, trucking along the row will preserve the four-square appearance of rectangular pictures, preventing keystoning.

Uses of the Arc

In an arcing shot, one keeps aimed at the subject while moving the camera mount in a curving path around the subject.

23   To progressively vary the angle from which a stationary subject is viewed . . .

23.1   . . . because it is interesting or informative to view it so.

Example: the subject is a statue, which has been designed to reveal a satisfying composition from many points of view.

23.2   . . . because one wishes to vary the picture on the screen to combat visual monotony without interrupting the continuity of the subject matter with a take.

Thus, one may arc around a grand piano during a long, continuous passage of music.

Fig. 15/1

24   To adjust the picture composition when the subjects change their physical relationship, and to do so without an abrupt change of shots.

For example, see *Figure 15/1*. Attention is on character A, who crosses B in the course of a long speech. As he crosses, the camera arcs in the opposite direction to keep a favorable angle on him.

25   To gradually direct attention to a new subject without the abruptness of a change of shots.

For example, see *Figure 15/2*. A and B are gossiping. During their conversation, it becomes progressively evident that they are being over-heard by C, who is the subject of their gossip.

26   To eliminate subject matter from the background.

Example: A and B are first shown conversing against the background of a crowd. As their conversation becomes more intimate, the camera grad-ually arcs around to show them against an inanimate background.

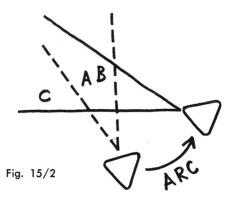

Fig. 15/2

Uses of the Zoom

The zoom may be used for approximately the same purposes as the dolly-in and dolly-back. There is one principal difference, however: In zooming, the size of the field expands and contracts, but there is no change in perspective relationships. For example, a figure in the foreground does not grow larger in proportion to a figure in the background as it would during a dolly-in. Also, because during a zoom the camera remains stationary, there is no change in the point of view. During a dolly-in, this change occurs. Thus, in *Figure 15/3,* more of the wall behind the door opening can be seen when the camera is dollied in.

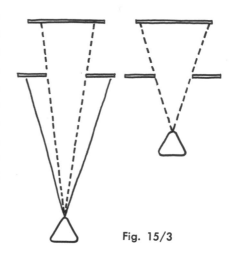

Fig. 15/3

In distinction to dolly shots, the zoom offers the following unique advantages:

27   To frame a shot exactly without having to change lenses or to move the camera forward or back to adjust framing.

This can save time between shots.

28   To vary the field as the subject expands or contracts, approaches or recedes, without having to move the camera or to cut to other cameras.

Hence:

29   To do a show on one camera, either to save the cost of extra camera operators, or to maintain a consistent subjective point of view—provided that:

The camera does not have to dolly to new positions while shooting, since this would require refocusing the range of the lens.

The subject matter can be properly framed within the widest and narrowest extremities of the lens angle.

The action is blocked to lead the camera logically and directly from one subject to another.

There is no need for subjects to be accented as they can be when suddenly revealed by the take to a new camera.

Subjects are arranged at such distances from camera as to prevent frequent and obvious zooming in and out, which can be very distracting for the viewer.

Each subject is so faced as to be viewed from the proper angle by the stationary camera.

The lens can be operated smoothly without perceptible jerks during the zooming.

30   To facilitate the pickup of programs where cameras must remain in fixed positions.

Zoom lenses are very useful in outdoor locations or in public halls where an audience is seated between the event and the camera positions.

31   To vary the size of the field without abruptly changing the point of view.

Thus, the zoom can preserve the unity of a single action such as a football play, which rapidly expands and contracts in the field of view. To cut to wider or narrower lenses and to different camera positions during the play can damage both the viewer's orientation and the continuity of the action. In tennis matches, taken from the margin of one court, one can zoom in as the ball is driven to the far court, thus avoiding the discontinuity of takes to another camera or the wig-wagging produced when a camera off one end of the net pans back and forth from court to court.

32   To eliminate the need for correlation between different cameramen during quickly expanding and contracting action by permitting this to be followed on one camera.

This is of obvious value during sports pickups.

33   To keep an advancing or receding subject framed at constant scale with less trouble than is sometimes encountered by a dolly-in or dolly-out.

In such instances, the zoom forestalls having to dolly over a rug or into furniture or into the field of another camera's shot.

It eliminates the need to follow focus and to risk going out of focus if the action is fast or varies in speed.

34 To alter the size of the field much more quickly than is possible by dollying.

Therefore:

34.1 To narrow attention rapidly to some detail which suddenly becomes urgently important.

The rapid zoom-in is one of the most forceful devices available to the director. Its impact can almost be that of a shock. In drama it may be used to support sudden, emotion-charged developments in the action. In hard-sell commercials it may serve to punch home some important point in the visual sales message. Quick, repeated zooming in and out has sometimes been used to induce a feeling of panic or other intense emotional excitement.

35 To keep at constant scale the subject matter framed during a pan over material which slants back obliquely in the camera field.

For example, with the camera in front of one end of a row of persons, a pan down the row on a standard lens will include progressively more persons, increasingly diminished in size. By zooming in during the pan, each person can be isolated in the frame and kept at the same screen size as the other persons.

36 To eliminate the exaggerated perspective which may occur when a camera dollies close to a subject on a wide-angle lens.

With a zoom, as previously explained, the perspective does not change.

37 To eliminate undesired changes in vertical angle, which may occur when a camera is dollied in close to a subject higher or lower than the level of the lens.

With a zoom, the point of view remains constant.

38 To keep a prompting device (fixed to the camera) at a constant distance from the performers.

Using a zoom lens to adjust framing obviously allows the camera to remain stationary. Hence the prompting device need not move away from the performers' range of vision as it would if the camera had to dolly back.

Chapter 16

The Director as Interpreter

1 Conform your choice and editing of shots to the meaning, mood and form of your program material.

Preserve the nature of your material as faithfully as you can despite its being obliged to pass through your cameras and microphones in order to reach its audience. As superintendent of this translation, you must make yourself a reliable interpreter.

2 To interpret the material faithfully, you must understand its purposes and characteristics.

To accurately translate the many subjects which television brings to the screen requires a keen sensibility and broad understanding of many more aspects of human activity than any book or course in directing could ever hope to encompass. So do not limit your study to the confines of studios and stations. Seek as many experiences as possible and meet them with an inquiring mind.

3 Camera treatment must vary according to the purpose of the subject matter.

3.1 For example, the purpose of instructional television is learning, not diversion or advertising.

Directors who fail to reflect this distinction in their work have been criticized by educators for pulling against the learning process in ways such as the following:

(1) Failure to understand that the student must demonstrate competence as the result of the lesson, which can't be all effortless, spoonfed entertainment. Excitement values should not be confused with methods of promoting understanding and ability. Suspense about the outcome of an experiment is not the same thing as realizing the principle which the experiment is intended to illustrate. Opening "teasers" and other "gimmicks" may not be in harmony with the purpose of the lesson. Cuts to human interest shots may interrupt the students' mental concentration.

(2) Failure to exhibit on the screen the proper learning stimulus because the director is not sufficiently knowledgeable in the subject area. Therefore, he may include irrelevant material in the picture, or only part of the relevant material—or he may introduce quite inappropriate material. For example, he may cut to a new visual stimulus during a listening experience, thus disturbing aural concentration; or he may urge the showing of pictures during the reading of a poem when the educational purpose is to develop the student's ability to cultivate his own images in response to verbal stimuli.

(3) Failure to exhibit the most effective learning stimuli because the director prefers to determine the shots by means of his own creative instincts rather than heeding the advice of learning psychologists or scientifically determining which of various visual approaches are most effective with a sample group of students.

(4) Failure to appreciate that a fast pace is not always conducive to learning. Thus, the director may not keep the camera on the learning stimulus long enough to permit comprehension, analysis or note taking. He may ignore the need for pauses designed to elicit student reactions such as thinking, investigating, problem-solving and practicing a new learning. In so doing, he has probably carried over from "showbusiness television" a notion that the lesson should be a one-way, sustained, fast-paced performance by the teacher, rather than a means whereby the teacher stimulates activity in the mind of the student.

(5) Failure to accommodate to the physical conditions of television reception in a classroom. This results in his not making images big enough and clear enough for the back row of a class of up to thirty students who are probably sharing the same receiver.

3.2   Commercials, on the other hand, require a different treatment.

If you are shooting a "hard sell" commercial where your purpose is to create a desire to buy, you may need to impress the potential customer's senses and emotions with forceful shots, filled with motion and frequent changes, which sweep him along with little time to question what has (or has not) been presented to him.

Certainly, you will want to be ever conscious (as some student directors are not) that the product and the sponsor's name should be shown to best advantage.

Yet not all commercials are identical in character. One which aims to portray the feminine allure which results from using a hair spray should not be staged and and shot like one which aims to portray the jangled nerves which can be avoided by drinking a caffein-free beverage.

3.3   The general purpose and character of the material should govern the treatment of the details.

For example, to create an atmosphere of feminine allure you will probably need to work with soft lighting, gentle curves and flowing transitions— whereas to create an impression of jangled nerves would presume percussive movements, angular composition, contrasty lighting, and abrupt transitions.

To make the details consistent, you first have to recognize the purpose and character of the whole.

But besides being faithful to the whole, you need to interpret the material point by point. Therefore:

4   Recognize, and support by individual picture statements, the changing points at each successive moment of the program material.

Always keep asking, "What is the point that I should be making at this moment?" Then make your picture support that point and no other. Follow the advice of Andreas Feininger, writing about the still photographer's picture story:

> The simpler the subject, the more direct the impression . . . In comparison to the eye, the lens sees too much . . . Rather than trying to say everything in one picture, subdivide complex subjects and setups and show them in the form of a short series in which each picture clearly illustrates only a single point—as a good writer prefers several short sentences to a single long and complicated one.[1]

[1] Andreas Feininger: *The Creative Photographer.* (Prentice-Hall, Inc., Englewood Cliffs, 1955) p. 290.

5   Recognize, and define by your pictorial treatment, the structural units of the material.

This applies to passages in music, figures in dance, paragraphs in speech, units in drama, plays in a sporting event and even to the succession of stories read by a news reporter. It also applies to such changes as between ending a song and beginning to talk, or between telling a humorous story and then pointing out cold fronts on a weather map.

5.1   Reinforce changes in the structure of the material by pronounced visual changes.

These visual changes can be accomplished by movement of the performers. Thus, to introduce a new topic, a performer can rise or sit or cross to a new location. He can pick up a property or lay one down. He can stop moving. He can turn from one center of attention to another. Devices such as these are constantly employed by actors. They are also useful when television teachers wish to emphasize the introduction of new ideas in their lessons.

The changes can also be made by camera movements. The camera can pan decisively from one subject to another, for instance, or it can dolly out to emphasize the end of a musical selection.

Most commonly, changes of pattern are marked by shot changes. These changes will be more decisive to the degree that there is a pronounced contrast of shot content—of screen size, perhaps, or of composition, or of subject. There will be little distinction between the news segment and the commercial which follows it if, as in one student director's exercise, both the news announcer and the commercial announcer are similarly framed and similarly attired, sitting at similar desks in front of similar backgrounds.

5.2   Correlate your shot changes with changes in the pattern of the program content; do not call them at random.

Example: During a piano selection, the director sees that the off-air cameraman has an interesting shot of the hammers hitting the strings. He likes it, so he takes it. Then the camera just released gets an equally fascinating shot of the pianist's reflection in the under side of the piano cover. The director cannot wait to show this to his public, so he takes this, too. His eyes have been busy, but his ears have been shut. Such randomly timed shots as these punctuate as falsely as do the periods in the following:

One phrase of the. Music ends and another. Begins then the selection. Finishes and the performer shifting. To talk announces. The title of his next selection he then starts. Playing again.

It sometimes helps to know the exact timing of each structural unit so that you'll be ready for a change when it occurs. When dealing with music of any appreciable length and complexity, it is advisable to follow a score on which shot changes and camera movements are marked at the appropriate measures.

5.3   Avoid breaking up the unity of a figure with unnecessary shots so that one can't see the forest for the trees.

By figure is meant a combination of elements (notes in music, for instance, or movements in a dance) which produces—unless you interfere with it—a single, complete, and distinct impression.

Ballet enthusiasts do not approve of the director who cuts in details of dancers' heads or feet or changes camera angles during some figure in which a constant and consistent view of the total bodily activity should be maintained. Devotees of serious music are irritated when a director changes his shot in the middle of a sustained musical phrase.

This kind of disruption is not confined to the arts. Suppose that a golf professional is demonstrating the technique of driving, which includes addressing the ball, the backswing, the downswing and the follow through. The director begins on a camera facing the demonstrator, but as the downswing commences he takes a camera facing in the direction of the drive. His motive, presumably, is to follow the flight of the ball down the fairway. This motive, however, is at odds with the purpose of the demonstration, which is to let viewers who are interested in improving their golfing form observe the continuity of the whole driving action. By cutting, the director has dissected this action and disoriented the observer.

To avoid taking new shots when the structure of the material fails to warrant it does not necessarily deprive you of all creative opportunity. For example, when shooting a pianist whose music lacks pronounced contrasts and changes, you can truck and dolly your camera to support crescendo and diminuendo, or merely to induce a pleasant sense of ongoing development.

5.4   If you have to change your subject during a sustained passage, use camera movement or dissolves, not takes.

As previously observed, a camera movement such as a dolly or pan moves smoothly and continuously from one subject to another. As a sustained movement, its appropriateness for supporting a sustained passage in the subject matter should be apparent. Contrasting with this is the take, appropriately known in motion pictures as the cut, which does indeed cut shots apart, making a sudden and complete cleavage between them, and being, therefore, unsatisfactory as a unifying device.

When you need to unify two separate shots, use the dissolve. With this device, the shots overlap and intermingle, blending together much as when one chemical substance dissolves in another.

Example: During an orchestral performance, the lead in developing a musical figure passes in succession from one instrument or group of instruments to another. Rather than stressing the introduction of new instruments, the director rightly chooses to preserve and clarify the structure of the music by sustaining the continuity of the figure. Therefore, he pans between the instruments if they are adjacent; or if they are not adjacent, he dissolves between them. Or if the passage begins on one instrument and includes progressively more instruments as it develops, the director will probably support this expansion with a dolly-back.

Another example: A lecturer on the humanities observes that, despite differences, the races of mankind have many qualities in common—whereupon there appears on the screen a series of still pictures, first of a Caucasian family, then a Negro family, then a Mongoloid family and so on. If the pictures are on slides, the director will dissolve between them. If they are enlargements mounted on poles in the studio, he will probably truck or dolly from one to another. Whether by gliding between them or blending them, he can help to stress their mutual association in the family of mankind. On the other hand, if the lecturer uses the sequence to emphasize differences between the races, the director should use takes to distinguish the subjects as separate entities.

6   Conform your pictorial transitions to those in the subject matter.

Because of its blending quality, the dissolve should be used to harmonize with program content which is itself marked by blended or gliding transitions. Although most kinds of program content are punctuated by changes which occur at precise instants and may therefore be appropriately accented by takes, a few evolve without marked breaks. For instance, there are the smoothly evolving movements of ice skaters, waltzers and fashion models. There is also the pianist who drifts through a selection of reveries or nocturnes, segueing from one to another. In such material there are no precise instants of change with which a take might appropriately coincide. Dissolves, however, change in the same manner as the content changes and can help to preserve its flow.

If, on the other hand, transitions within a sequence are not blended in the manner just described, do not dissolve between them. For example, in televising a singer you wish to go from a medium shot to a closeup at the end of a musical phrase. A take in this case will make a "clean" transition. A dissolve will be "sloppy," since it begins in one phrase and ends in another.

6.1   Consider the degree to which changes occur in the material, and regulate accordingly the degree of contrast between one shot and another.

Action which is violent or which contains sudden reversals and big surprises demands pronounced contrast between shot and shot. But in a love scene where everything—girl, moonlight and murmured words—is soft and pretty, the contrast between shots should be much more restrained.

Pertinent here is the following note to a student director: "To cut from a long shot to a closeup during a gentle, ongoing action such as that of the guitar vocalist's melancholy refrain is too abrupt. One needs an intermediate waist shot or a gradual dolly-in. A sudden change of scale would serve to reinforce a change of selection from dreamy ballad, say, to bellowed rock-and-roll, but in the content at hand all musical transitions are very gradual."

7   Reflect the degree of animation in the action by the pace of your visual changes.

The slower and more quiet the scene, the more restricted can be the performers' movement and the frequency of shot changes. Increasing animation is usually reflected by bolder, quicker, and more frequent movements by the performers. It can also be supported by increasing the rate of cutting.

8   Show by your camera treatment whether the subjects are allied or opposed.

Alliance between two subjects can be reinforced by maintaining them in the same shot with more or less equal attention on each. Thus, you would maintain a shared shot of two entertainers as they perch side by side on stools, claiming long friendship and reminiscing about their past experiences together.

Opposition can be reinforced by taking the subjects in separate one-shots or by cutting between reverse-angle shots. Such treatment is appropriate, for example, in drama when two characters are in conflict, or in music to contrast two opposing musical statements, or in a contest show to reinforce the sense of competition.

9   Harmonize your camera treatment with any exaggerated or distorted effects in the material.

In plays of the thriller type, for instance, the characters are apt to be boldly drawn and contrasted. There are swiftly developing complications, sudden reversals of fortune, and situations which are magnified and intense. For corresponding camera treatment, the director may use unusual camera angles, sudden pans and zooms, abrupt takes between contrasting shot content, and wide angle lenses to exaggerate the speed and force of developing danger.

10   Use your cameras to build up the increasing tension of a situation.

To create dramatic tension is to build up the dynamic potential of an event, meanwhile delaying its occurrence, thereby generating excitement in the audience but delaying its release. The technique resembles stretching a rubber band or increasing the difference in charge between the plates of an electric capacitor.

10.1   Build tension through suspense.

Keep the camera off a subject while desire to see it is being built up.

Begin by showing only part of a subject, then dolly back to reveal it by degrees.

Pan across neutral territory towards a subject, then pan onto it, revealing it by degrees.

10.2   Build tension by using your cameras to point up in turn the forces and elements which are about to become engaged.

Thus, in a baseball game, before a crucial pitch, show the pitcher hesitating; show the runners waiting near each base, ready to steal to the next one.

Thus, in a circus act, show the high-wire artist on his aerial perch; then the height and thinness of the wire he will attempt to cross.

**11   Regulate the forcefulness of your picture statements to the rela-
tive degrees of importance in the program material.**

*11.1   Recognize that some parts of the program are more important
that others.*

Special stress, for instance, is needed for the introductory appearance
of subjects which are assuming a dominant role in the action. For example,
the host of a children's program, saying, "Now, let's see what's in our mystery box," moves away from camera towards a box in the background,
which appears very small and insignificant in relation to everything else in
the frame. This is what should not be. As the new center of attention, the
box has received insufficient visual stress.

In drama, special stress is needed for key lines and actions, i.e. those
which epitomize character, delineate the contending forces or are major
developments of the plot. It is also needed for crises and for the climax,
where the major forces engage in a decisive encounter from which results
the final state of equilibrium.

Similarly, important statements are to be found in speeches, in music
and in many other kinds of program material.

In all dynamically constructed material there is a pattern of crescendo
and diminuendo, of increasing force followed by relaxation. Within a given
line of development, new material must be more impressive than that which
preceded it in order to maintain interest. Thus, a variety act progresses in
the direction of the increasingly skillful or spectacular, and a scene in
drama towards accumulated meaning or a more complicated situation or
stronger assertions of action or emotion. When one line of development has
reached its end, there is usually some relaxation as a new line of development begins. But overall, the various lines of development themselves
mount to a climax where the program attains its highest level of importance
and aims to exert the strongest impression on its audience.

Having ascertained the degrees of importance in your material, portray them with picture statements of appropriate force.

*11.2   A picture statement will be more forceful to the degree that it
economizes the viewer's attention.*

Writing on the analogous subject of force in language, Herbert Spencer
made this useful observation:

> Regarding language as an apparatus of symbols for the convey-
> ance of thought, we may say that, as in a mechanical apparatus, the

more simple and better arranged its parts, the greater will be the effect produced. In either case, whatever force is absorbed by the machine is deducted from the result. A reader or listener has at each moment but a limited amount of mental power available. To recognize and interpret the symbols presented to him requires part of this power; to arrange and combine the images suggested requires a further part; and only that part which remains can be used for realizing the thought conveyed. Hence the more time and attention it takes to receive and understand each sentence, the less time and attention can be given to the contained idea; and the less vividly will that idea be conceived.[1]

In visual communication, as already discussed in connection with the Moment-by-Moment Questionnaire, economy of attention can be achieved by arranging the parts of the picture to be easily read as a whole, isolated from distracting and irrelevant information.

In progressing from picture to picture, a common way to isolate a subject for more forceful attention is to move from a group shot to a one-shot of it, either by taking the one-shot or by having the subject move away from the group, with the camera following the move. For still more force, one can concentrate attention closely on the most expressive features of the subject, either by taking a closeup, by panning or dollying into a closeup, or by having the subject itself move into a closeup.

11.3   A picture statement will be more forceful to the degree that its active content impinges on the viewer.

As a general rule, a speaker's words will seem more forceful to the degree they are directed towards camera. Thus, by changing from a balanced two-shot to reverse over-shoulder shots of an arguing couple, one can move the television viewer into the field of fire, so to speak, so that each character's emotion impinges on him more directly and forcefully.

The closer a subject appears to the viewer, the more forceful it will be. When a person is speaking directly to camera, an especially important remark can be reinforced by having him move closer to camera to deliver it. Even when the audience is not being addressed directly, it is accepted in television as in the theatre that the strongest move a performer can make is one directed towards the audience.

11.4   A picture statement will be more forceful to the degree that anticipation has been created for it.

Examples of this principle have already been cited. For instance, after

[1] Herbert Spencer: *Philosophy of Style.* (Pageant Press, N.Y., 1959) p. 17.

the master of ceremonies has introduced a concert pianist, the camera pans briefly across the foreshortened, raised lid of the piano before the pianist comes into view. The slight delay builds anticipation, which adds importance to the artist's appearance.

You will remember also how, in commercials, anticipation is sometimes raised by creating imbalance in the frame. The camera is panned to leave one side of the screen empty; then the blank space is filled with some important visual message.

One can also leave the new subject outside the frame until anticipation for it has been created. To have it in view before its turn to enter the action is to deny it the impact of "making an entrance."

11.5   A picture statement will be more forceful to the degree that its appearance constitutes a pronounced change from what has just preceded it.

Familiarity and sameness dull attention, but viewers will attend strongly to something different from what they have been experiencing. Hence, to impress them with the importance of a subject, introduce it by means of some pronounced visual change. Thus, have a performer rise, move, stop, or turn to deliver some important remark. Or take a new shot substantially different from the preceding one. A take has the power to say, "Look, something new and important is happening."

At least, it will say this provided that it follows a shot which has been sustained for some appreciable duration. Takes, like other devices, lose their force when repeated too constantly. Hence, avoid using them simply because your subjects are too far apart to be included in the same frame. Don't separate the hostess and her guest so widely that, when they are chatting over tea, you must cut to the hostess when she asks, "One lump or two?", and then to the guest when she replies, "Two, please." Save your takes for things that matter.

To bring out the force of excitement in a fast sequence of brief shots, precede them by a shot of much longer duration. To make a series of close-ups effective, precede them with one or more looser shots.

A subject seen constantly on one camera is liable to lose its impact. By showing something different on the screen, if only for a few moments, impact can be restored to the subject when the camera returns to it again.

When movement is involved, either by the subject or by the camera, force increases with both the speed and the degree of the change. For example, by magnifying both speed and enlargement, a wide-angle lens increases the force of an oncoming car or train.

11.6   In applying visual force, support the climactic order.

Don't exhaust your emphatic devices through overuse before the climax has been attained.

Don't shoot in the direction of anti-climax. For example, when shooting a trumpeter, don't start with tight closeups of his fingering and embouchure, the perspiration on his face and the glint in his eye—and then back away into long shots. Another example: If you introduce a trio of performers by progressively dollying back from a shot of one of them, the second person, being smaller on the screen, has less impact than the first, and the third person is weaker still.

Know your objective. If you wish to pan across a line of military tanks which are passing in review, which is the more climactic direction in which to pan? By starting close on the nearest tank and widening the shot, you are stressing the vast armament which the country possesses. By starting wide and panning onto the tread of the nearest tank, you are emphasizing the relentless, crushing power of this type of war machine.

11.7   Suit your force to the occasion.

By regulating the force of your visual treatment, you control the degree to which an idea or event or emotion is impressed on your viewer, and that degree should be proportionate to the significance which you wish to convey. Too much force results in bombast—defined by Herbert Spencer as "a force of expression too great for the magnitude of the ideas embodied." Therefore, don't be like the director who shoots every interview in his sports program by cropping the participants at the hairline and the chin. On the other hand, as Hamlet says, "Be not too tame, neither." Don't shoot everything so loosely that your visual statements are indecisive and pointless.

12   In expressing the nature of your material, encourage and do not inhibit the expressive abilities of your performers.

As previously stated in this book, audiences do not tune in to see your camera shots, but rather to see human beings doing something. And human beings, although some directors may be reluctant to admit it, are capable of infinitely more expression than are camera shots. Particularly in televising drama, it is wise to begin by determining what human movements and relationships are natural and appropriate to the circumstances, letting these play the lead, as it were, and the cameras the accompaniment.

The more you use your performers for emphasizing points, directing attention from one to another, and changing the picture composition through their movements, the more you can save your shot changes for moments when they really count.

Chapter 17

Examples of Interpretation

This chapter contains notes written by the author as critiques of student-directed exercises. These notes should help to illustrate and reinforce many of the principles which were presented in the preceeding chapter.

Poetry Reading

I'm going to select Chris' exercise as an example of some of the director's concerns in communicating his material. The exercise consisted of his sister reading excerpts from Edna St. Vincent Millay (lyric poetry, feminine and somewhat sad), talking briefly to introduce each excerpt, then reading it from a book in her hand.

What Chris did:

He realized that mood was important and that the poetry was "dematerialized," a matter of the heart and spirit rather than of physical objects. Accordingly, he found an appropriate musical theme and used a simple, tasteful title card. He set his reader on a simple, high stool against a plain two-fold flat. He wanted his shooting sequence to support the structure of the program. Therefore, he used one shot for introductions and another for reading the excerpts. He resisted cutting between the cameras during the excerpts since there was no motivation in the material for so doing and since a camera change would create in the viewer a new physical awareness which could disturb his concentration on the poetry.

What I suggested:

What part of the scene carries the visual expression?

In this case, it was subtle shadings of expression in the performer's face and eyes, which were too distant in Chris' shots to easily discern. Much of the physical material which he included in the frame was inert and inexpressive—also distracting (the lavalier cord and the highlighted knees seen at the bottom of the shot used for introductions). Therefore, I suggested that he make both shots proportionately closer: a waist shot for the introductions and a shoulder shot for reading the poetry.

Is the expressive quality properly supported?

(1) The background seemed to be too sharply focused for the "dematerialized" feeling of the poetry. Therefore, I suggested that it be placed farther behind the performer and that the cameras move back and use longer lenses to place the background outside the depth of field.

(2) I studied the lighting. As Chris had it, the key light was frontal on the poetry reading shot, illuminating the features symmetrically and uniformly. On the introduction shots it was falling from an angle, modeling the face with soft shadow, which would have helped the mood of the poetry. Therefore, I suggested that he reverse his shots camera for camera.

(3) Then I proposed that he have his performer face a little to the side for the poetry reading. This was done for several reasons. First, it improved the lighting distribution, insuring that a triangular patch of light fell so as to illuminate her right eye. Secondly, the informal balance seemed to make her features more attractive and the pictorial composition more in harmony with Millay's poetic style than a stiff symmetrical arrangement. Thirdly, I asked myself, "Where should audience attention be during the poetry reading?" and answered, "On the poetry—not staring into the reader's eye.'"

(4) Between shots I suggested that Chris use dissolves, which would let the savor of the poetry die out more slowly.

Can the performance itself be improved?

The reader puckered her brow periodically as she read—a sign of strain or a mannerism which the director should have tried to eliminate. Remember, you work on perfecting the performance as well as the shots. The performance is what the viewers notice and care about.

This was ostensibly a rather simple show, but notice how many details of expression were involved. That's why I recommend that you stick to short exercises, so there's time to work on improving them.

A Piano Pickup

Terry's piano pickup was commendably faithful to the structure of the pianist's selection.

It had unity: at the opening (*Figure 17/1*) he dollied out from a shot of the strings and at the end he returned to the same shot, thus signifying unmistakable finality.

It had variety, moving out (shot "a") from the strings to the whole piano, then arcing through a varied angle. Next, shot "b" from a new angle moved from a full shot of the pianist into a closeup of his hands and back to a full shot again. Then "c", from a reverse angle, dollied from a full shot into the same closeup of strings seen at the beginning.

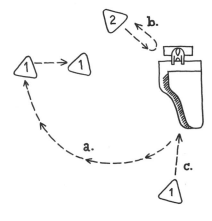

Fig. 17/1

It had development: it grew and then diminished in keeping with the pattern of the music, reaching its climax some four-fifths of the way through with shot "b's" closest approach to the hands. The take from shot "a" to "b" occurred at a pronounced change in the music. The dolly-in during "b" accompanied a crescendo, during which the hands of the player became more active and interesting to watch. The dolly-back from these hands accompanied a musical diminuendo. The change to shot "c" also occurred at a change in the musical structure, but since it was musically a rather blended change, the camera change was a dissolve rather than a take.

All this, at least, is what Terry intended. In practice, he found that it takes time to pace camera moves to the duration of the musical passages. On the first run-through the arcing movement of shot "a" went too fast. The camera reached its destination too early; so we waited until time for shot "b" with a static picture, during which interest started to wane.

Preparing a Child's Hospital Breakfast Tray

This exercise illustrated some useful principles:

To have only one camera ever show the demonstrator's face meant that she only needed to look towards one camera. This helped to relax her by making things simple for her. It also meant a consistent visual orientation for the viewer.

Props were shown by themselves in a cleared area before being added to the other objects on the tray. Thus, they made a full impression on us, since we did not have to divide our attention between them and several other attractions in the frame.

The closeup camera and display arrangements were so related that, without a lens change, objects were always framed at the correct size—the tray, as the largest item, being farther from camera than the area where objects were seen before being placed on the tray.

One change of placement was made. On the first run-through, the girl's arm reached up close to camera to get slices of toast, then moved backward with them to place them on a small plate farther from camera. As revised, the hand picked up toast from close to the demonstrator, then advanced it towards camera to place it on the plate. This was an improvement for several reasons:

(1) The strongest move is one towards camera; the approaching subject grows in size, taking more and more command of the frame, reaching a climax when the movement ceases, the subject having gained its greatest magnification. In the first run-through, the advancing movement was that of an empty hand, the climax occurring as it procured a piece of toast in the foreground; thereafter, the receding movement of the toast to the plate was in an anticlimactic direction. In the second run-through, the climax occurred as it should, at the moment of placing the toast on the plate.

(2) The first run-through required two movements of the arm, forward and back in a kind of hook pattern. The revision required only one deft, concise advance of the hand to accomplish the business. Grace comes from economy of effort. So does force. Always work to make one motion do the work of two.

(3) In the first run-through, when the arm withdrew, the plate was too small in the frame. Moving the plate closer to camera gave it the dominance it needed as the subject of the shot.

A Guitar-Playing Ballad Singer

Never having heard his vocalist's selection, Bud's problem was to work out shots and transitions which would suit its mood, which turned out to be lonesome, and its tempo, which was sustained and drifting. He discovered that close shots of the bright, evenly lighted face were less effective than those which showed the shadowed sides of the figure and included a little lonely-feeling dark space around it. Takes, he found, were too abrupt for the drift of the opening and closing segments, and sudden changes from wide to tight framing fought against the rather even tenor of the piece. He also discovered that these opening and closing sections offered no interesting fingering of guitar strings to justify a closeup. As time for the exercise ran out, he was beginning to discover that there was a middle section of the song which, being stronger and brighter in feeling with more vigorous chords, might have provided a variation in camera treatment. The moral: Although one sometimes has to shoot a number like this ad lib, your camerawork will be far more appropriate if you know the mood and structure of the music in advance.

Pantomime Face Panel Quiz
(Excerpts from the Critique)

One of the first duties in shooting a contest is to establish a sense of opposition between the contestants. In the introduction, single shots of each contestant alone would have done more to set up the contest. Remember the fight announcer's "In this corner . . . and in this corner . . ."

To simply keep alternating between the three-shot and the pantomime face which the panelists were trying to identify did too little to promote the excitement of the contest. Intercutting between the various faces would have livened up the game—not only because of the increased visual variety, but also because more action and interaction result from seeing elements isolated in sequence: first the stimulus, then the response; first an action, then a reaction. This method raises anticipation, then pays it off. It isolates each subject for increased concentration, thus giving it greater impact. It comes in close enough to let one appreciate the facial expressions—the perplexity, the dawning realizations, etc., which are strong interest factors that you can't afford to throw away. Intercutting promotes interplay, the exciting quality of give-and-take.

A Commercial for Contact Lenses

In this one eyes were most important. The girl announcer should have been chosen for the warmth and vitality of her eyes. The lighting crew might have worked at the special task of giving her eyes a sparkle. Framing was too loose at first; her turn into profile, saying, "You can't tell that I'm wearing contact lenses," didn't make sense since we weren't close enough to tell anyway.

The painting which was defocused to show how blurry things can look without lenses was done in an Impressionist technique without defined contours and therefore continued to look rather blurred even after it had been focused back in.

Always keep asking, "What is the point I'm trying to get across at this particular moment?" (E.g., to show how much sharper things look with proper lenses; to show that one can't detect when contact lenses are being worn; to show that contact lenses preserve the natural appeal of a girl's eyes, etc.) Then make each point as positively as you can.

Drygas Commercial

Zero in more and more on what really matters. This is particularly important at the end of a sales pitch, where you want to finish off with a strong, lasting impression.

At the end of the Drygas commercial, Ted had already held up a can of Drygas in a hip shot. Then he produced a can of windshield spray from his pocket, saying, "While you're there, also get a can of . . . etc." And that was the finish, with both products very distant, competing for attention with a door, trees, and a bold-patterned overcoat. Result: no IMPACT! Furthermore, the cans stayed held in his hands for several seconds without anything happening to them, which meant that they were constantly getting weaker as an interest factor.

So we had Ted walk towards camera with them, holding them somewhat forward and almost at a height with his face. As he approached, more and more competing elements disappeared from the frame; the products got larger and larger; and they also got into sharp focus compared with his face, which got softer because of the narrowing depth of field. Furthermore, because Ted was bearing down on us, concentrating more and more on each of us as an individual customer, his persuasion heightened. More and more we could feel our contact with him, see the detail in his eyes which said, "I'm very earnest about this and I'm talking to *you!*"

Remember: action must have either crescendo or diminuendo to keep it from growing tedious. In brief and urgent messages like commercials it's usually crescendo that counts. Don't keep things so-so. Make them *more so!*

A Scene from "The Glass Menagerie"

Know the meaning you want to convey at each point in the action. Then visualize pictures which will best convey this meaning. Then try to have the cameras in the right places to convey the meanings, one after another.

For instance, you want to convey the feeling that a boy and girl are having an awkward time getting together. Maybe space them apart on a longish seat, start on a shot of him and then pan across space to her, thus emphasizing their separation.

You want to point up the girl's enthusiasm about her little glass unicorn. Therefore shoot close, so that people can see the light in her eyes and the little, shining, fragile object in her hand.

You want to contrast the boy's physical energy with her shrinking, static posture. So perhaps shoot past her, seated in the foreground, to the full figure of the boy dancing by himself to the music of the cafe across the street.

You want to show her gathering courage to accept his invitation to dance. Maybe we could look down towards her over his shoulder, ultimately to see her rising to him.

The spell is broken when the unicorn is knocked off the table and broken. Surely a cut here will stress the abruptness of the calamity and change of mood—but if the abruptness is to be felt by the audience, you will need to have refrained from cutting for some time before this moment; otherwise the device will have been exhausted from overuse.

To mark the moment strongly, try cutting from a long shot of them dancing together to a closeup of the girl's face as she registers dismay at the sound of the breaking glass. Then cut away to his face, looking concerned. The first cut makes an extreme contrast of scale; the second, a total change of picture content. Try audio contrast also, by having the music end with the first cut and by having neither of them say anything while the two close-ups are taken.

These are *my* visions. You, of course, may have your own interpretations; but the essential thing is that you *have* interpretations and that you be able to justify them from a thorough analysis of the action.

Then you realize your interpretations in terms of human movement and camera treatment. Get your characters to move. (That's life. That's the show.) And then get your cameras to follow them, panning, booming up or down, widening or narrowing the frame, changing the angle and frame content as may be necessary. As long as the characters are active, the audience will not notice what the camera is doing—as long as its moves are motivated by the action of the characters.

In this connection, ask more of your cameras than you do. In the scene just described I tried to show what a pedestal mount could accomplish—operated by a girl, no less:

Camera on 2″ lens, pedestaled down to the girl's seated level, looks past her to the boy and the lighted cafe sign through the window . . .

pans right to follow the boy as he dances by himself . . .

booms way up and dollies in as he comes forward, so that we look down over his shoulder to the girl, who eventually rises up towards us . . .

and into his arms—the camera meanwhile tilting up to bring more of his head into the shot . . .

then simultaneously booming down and dollying back as she tries some tentative steps with him.

 As the camera is backing one way, they back the other into a long shot which shows how she lets herself go into broad motion.

Then cut as the unicorn breaks!

Note the changes in composition achieved by the characters' movements—the characters leading and the cameras playing the accompanying harmony to their movement.

Breaking the Suspect's Alibi

Tuesday evening we made considerable revisions in a little scene during which a police inspector grilled a suspect with little success until he finally produced an incriminating document which forced a confession.

In the first version there was a little physical activity to begin with when the suspect entered the office and approached the inspector's desk, but thereafter nothing happened but a monotonous succession of reverse angle shots. Besides being dully repetitive, these shots failed to establish the changing points in the encounter and its overall construction.

Here's the structure of the piece as I see it. It starts rather slowly and deliberately with the two men first meeting and sizing up each other. Then it intensifies with an exchange of questions and answers which gets the inspector nothing but frustration. Next comes a change: the inspector gets inspired for a new attack, which leads to his disclosure of the paper. This brings the climax: the suspect confesses.

One has to point up these changes—particularly the climax, towards which the whole action is driving. The first version failed to point up the changes for two principal reasons:

(1) There was not enough opportunity for varied expression by the performers, because they were nailed down to fixed positions.

(2) There was insufficiently varied expression in the camera treatment.

Here's how we tried to overcome these difficulties:

Reverse angle shots were quite appropriate during the exchange of questions and answers. To restrict them to this exchange and protect their effectiveness there, we decided to precede them with a sustained opening shot. After them, we decided to have the inspector rise from his desk chair, both to emphasize his frustration and to give him more physical latitude for pressing home his winning attack. As outcome of this attack, the suspect's confession could be supported by taking a close one-shot of him, but to give this take sufficient impact we decided to precede it by a sequence sustained on one camera. So the resulting shot pattern became:

Suspect's entrance and
move to desk .... One camera
First round of questions
and alibis .... Reverse angle shots
Inspector's frustration .... A rise
Inspector's successful
attack .... One camera, broader movement
Suspect's confession .... Take to a close one-shot

I particularly welcomed being able to work with the two passages on one camera for another reason besides those already cited. To change your picture content and to make new points, most of you rely wholly on taking new shots. I wanted to show you that new points can still be made and the composition varied even while remaining on one camera. To remind you of this, I've sketched a rough story-board of the entire camera treatment. Read this in connection with the floor plan (*Figure 17/2*). On that plan the dash line shows the approximate path of the inspector after his exasperated rise.

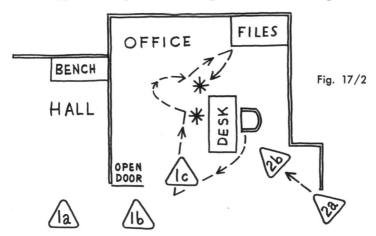

Fig. 17/2

The asterisks indicate approximate locations of the suspect after he has entered the office.

Now, here are the picture statements:

(1) Camera 1, from position 1a, shoots office door.

(2) Inspector emerges a step or two into hall, looks to camera left and beckons, motivating camera 1 to pan left, revealing . . .

(3) . . . the suspect, seated on bench at end of hall. Inspector exits from frame back to his desk, leaving door open.

(4) Suspect rises and moves forward towards door, thereby enlarging on screen so that we get a close look at his face. He enters office, camera 1 dollying after him until . . .

(5) . . . it reaches a two-shot, during which inspector goes behind his desk, sits, and fires his first question. This shot is repeated a few times, alternating with . . .

(6) . . . a reverse angle shot taken by camera 2 from position 2a. The first take emphasizes the suspect's claim: "I don't know anything about it."

(7) Exasperated from getting nowhere with his line of questioning, inspector rises (on camera 1), moves around camera right end of desk into a closeup, which registers his inspiration for a new attack.

(8) He swoops in on suspect, camera 1 dollying after him at the same pace into position 1c. (Camera 2 can now move to position 2b in order to be ready for its next shot.)

(9) Not having received the answer he expects, inspector strides to camera left, camera 1 panning with him as he halts, turns, and swoops back right again . . .

(10) this time to confront suspect from the side.

(11) Then he moves back to filing cabinet, leaving suspect in foreground. He finds the paper he wants and . . .

(12) comes forward to wave the incriminating document under the suspect's nose, camera 1 simultaneously moving in on the suspect from the opposite direction.

(13) Take 2, from position 2b, for a big closeup of suspect as he confesses.

Notice how each of the preceding picture statements makes its own definite point:

(1) tells where we are.

(2) introduces the inspector and creates suspense: he's ready for someone.

(3) pays off who the someone is to a degree, but plays on our desire to see him closer. Gives promise of some kind of interaction between the someone and the inspector.

(4) enlarges our visual acquaintance with the someone; also, by revealing the uncertainty with which he enters the door, further arouses our curiosity about what is to happen.

(5) sets up the confrontation and points up the opening question, thus starting the conflict which is the main subject of the scene.

(6), alternating with (5), reinforce the opposition between the two characters. (Remember that these were practically the only shots used in the original run-through.)

(7) ends the first round of questioning with the inspector's rise and points up his determination (seen in closeup) to go for a second round.

(8) uses a camera movement in towards the suspect in order to reinforce the inspector's attack, and also in order to view the second round more closely than the first round, thus helping to build towards the climax.

(9) helps to make the second round more active and urgent by allowing the inspector freer movement. This movement varies the composition by carrying him away from the suspect into a one-shot. It gives more impact to his next question by getting the suspect out of the picture momentarily. This renews interest in the suspect when he does enter the picture again. It also obviously allows the inspector to move in on the suspect again.

(10) illustrates what has been explained in the three preceding sentences.

(11) uses a strong movement in depth to introduce and point up the filing cabinet, whence issues the document which wins the round.

(12) is, so to speak, a squeeze play, with the inspector moving in on the victim from one direction and the camera moving in on him from the other. The converse camera movement has the effect of intensifying the inspector's movement, which, being straight towards camera, is already a strong one. The moves result in a tight two-shot, which permits the significant document to be as large as possible in the frame.

(13) is, of course, the take to a big image of the suspect's face, to give maximum force to his confession.

I hope you'll understand from this example how changes of picture can support changes of meaning from moment to moment, adding not merely visual variety, but also a variety of understanding which makes the viewer's experience more perceptive and more dynamic.

Camera Treatment for a String Quartet

Although not a critique of a student exercise, this final example is still *à propos*. It is a list of shooting principles which were used in video recording the performances of a string quartet:

Dissolve during the more legato and lyrical passages. During the more staccato and dramatic ones use takes.

In general, use takes to separate one passage from another. Within a passage, if shots of different picture content have to be taken, unify them with dissolves. Pan or truck when the lead for sustaining the passage passes from one instrument to another. For crescendo and diminuendo, dolly in and out.

When you do dolly out to support a portion that is louder and more dynamic, boom up and shoot down as much as possible in order to fill the frame with the activity of the musicians, since a low angle shows too much of the motionless background. An alternative to the dolly-backs for very agitated portions is to get close to single instrumentalists and then pan from one to another.

The symmetry of the frontal group shot does not seem as active as those taken from side angles.

The greater the contrast in musical content between one passage and another, the greater should be the contrast in shot content—in angle, for instance, or screen size of the visual subject matter.

For especially dramatic passages, try close-in shots with a 50mm lens from a low camera position or by using the periscope with a low mirror reflection. These will increase the contrast in size between foreground and background figures, supporting the dynamic contrasts in the music.

Chapter 18

Stimulating Responses

1 Stimulate your viewers. Make and keep them responsive to your program.

Think of yourself as working not merely on a program but on an audience. What passes through your cameras is only a means to an end. What you are really programming is a sequence of active responses in the organisms of your viewers, in their minds, emotions, and motor mechanisms. Think, then, of the program which you are directing as a series of stimuli designed to elicit audience responses.

2 These stimuli should be visual as well as aural.

The presence of a screen leads your viewers to expect stimulation for their eyes as well as their ears. Unless they have been warned in some fashion not to expect much visual stimulation and are prepared to feel rewarded primarily by what they hear, the lack of visual information will make them inattentive and apathetic.

3 The visual stimuli should satisfy two primary conditions:

3.1 They should be definite, positive, and pointed.

An organism tends to respond to only one stimulus at a time. The stimulus must be sufficiently pronounced to provoke a response and sufficiently definite to elicit the response intended. Therefore, as you were advised at the outset of this book, learn to perceive your program content as a series of changing points. Convey each point by means of its own separate picture statement, making that statement as positive as possible and as forceful as its significance warrants.

3.2   The visual stimuli should keep changing.

A constant set of conditions does not act as a stimulus; a stimulus is always a change. In a static visual situation (e.g. when a still photograph is on camera), the viewer's interest drains away as soon as the pertinent information has been exhausted. As a director, you must keep cranking up interest as you would an old spring-driven phonograph. To do this, keep giving the viewer new meaningful visual information. Keep showing him new things to notice and react to.

4   Induce visual change through your camera treatment.

4.1   Keep new visual subjects out of sight until their turn comes to enter the action.

Remember how, in Chapter 2, this was done with the guest violinist and also with his violin.

4.2   Find camera positions which provide maximum shot variety.

For an example, you may wish to look ahead to Chapter 22 ("Making Floor Plans"), noting Fig. 22/9 and the story-board derived from it.

4.3   Between shots, when time permits, don't be reluctant to move cameras to locations which permit new shot possibilities.

This may become particularly desirable when a group of performers remains in fixed position for an appreciable length of time.

4.4   When animation is restricted to only a portion of the subject, shoot close enough to make that animation discernible.

For example, if a lecturer remains stationary and does not express himself with gestures, shoot close enough to at least reveal the changes in his facial expression.

4.5   As soon as the closeup of an inanimate subject has made its point, go back to the shot of a human being.

In entertainment television, this may happen in as little as three seconds. In educational television, however, more time in closeup may be needed for a studied examination of the material.

4.6   To enliven a lengthy shot of a static subject, consider the possibilities of camera movement.

Can you dolly in to contract and concentrate the interest? Dolly out to expand the field of interest? Pan from one part of the subject to another? Arc around it for a progressively changing view? When contemplating such possibilities, however, remember that noticeable camera movements should have a reason that is evident to the viewer.

5   Prefer animated visuals to static ones.

For example, use pull strips on bar charts to make the bars mount one after another. Use them to make a route travel across a map. Use them (as mentioned in Chapter 1) to reveal in succession the Five Rules of Water Safety.

Use magnetic boards which allow the performer to add and remove pieces and move them from one place to another.

Instead of merely talking about inanimate objects, show them in action. How dull it was in one student exercise to watch the performer point out the parts of a violin as it lay inertly on a table. How much livelier (and more informative) to see him pick it up, pluck a string, tighten a peg, tuck the instrument under his chin to demonstrate the shoulder rest, etc. Similarly, to assemble a rifle or take it apart is more interesting than to merely point out the parts of the assembled piece.

When citing statistics, business with concrete objects can be more interesting than abstract charts. For example, to show that the wheat flour consumed in England comes 10% from Great Britain, 16% from the Sterling Areas, and 66% from the Western Hemisphere, one might slice a loaf of bread into the relative proportions.

5.1   Some ways of animating still pictures are more appropriate to film techniques than to electronic cameras.

Fast zooms or quickly changing shots of the details of a still visual, particularly one of small dimensions, are likely to require the use of a film camera and an animation stand for professional results. For information, consult a book on film techniques.

6 Introduce change through performers' business.

Again remember: the audience isn't interested in camera shots. What it wants to see is something happening to the subject of a shot—and it's your responsibility to make this happen.

Even when performers remain in fixed locations, you can still work to give them changing and expressive business.

For example, in a toothbrush commercial as devised by a student director, the salesman sat behind a desk doing nothing but hold the toothbrush while he (1) remarked that the previous act on this show had been a good one, (2) introduced the toothbrush, and (3) recited its claimed advantages. This was revised as follows:

SALESMAN:
(SEATED SIDEWISE, LOOKING OFF CAMERA) Boy, that was great, wasn't it! etc.

(TURNING TO CAMERA) I want to show you something else that's great . . .

(LIFTING TOOTHBRUSH FROM DESK TOP) . . . and here it is: the Dent-87 toothbrush.

(RUNNING FINGERS OVER BRISTLES) The only brush made out of genuine Toughlon, the fibre that stands up and springs back and never wilts.

(RAISING ENDORSEMENT CARD BEHIND BRUSH) Dent-87 is backed by the Loomis Laboratory Seal—and do you know why?

(EXTENDING BRUSH TOWARDS CAMERA) Let's take a closer look . . . etc.

Each line brings a visual change and new business. One way to judge a television script is to count the number of stage directions. Inside the parentheses of the above revision are the factors which make a good television performance instead of "radio on camera."

7 Induce visual change through perfomers' movements from place to place.

It is worth repeating: don't freeze your performers into blocked out positions merely so they can be sitting ducks for your camera shots. Resist inhibiting them with too many technical prescriptions. Instead, recognize and promote the important role which human movement plays in communicating meaning and in maintaining interest through changing visual stimulation. Examples of this have been given, particularly in the "Drygas Commercial" and "Breaking the Suspect's Alibi" in Chapter 17.

7.1   Study the language of human movement and changing physical relationships.

For acquiring command of this language, theatrical experience is invaluable.

Do you know how actors control attention and regulate emphasis through movement and gesture?

Do you realize the difference between moving with breadth and moving with restraint? . . . between agitation and composure? . . . between quick movements and slow ones?

What does it mean: to rise? . . . to sink down? . . . to confront someone? . . . to turn your back on someone? . . . to approach a person? . . . to move away? . . . to pursue? . . . to stop and turn?

Test yourself on these questions by providing stage directions for the following speeches. What are He and She doing in the course of their dialogue? When are they together? When apart? Do you see any occasions for confrontation? . . . evasion? . . . pursuit? . . . turnings   towards   or away? . . . halted movement? (The speeches, by the way, make no pretense to dramatic quality. They were written by a student expressly to serve in the classroom the same purpose as here.)

SHE: All right. Now we're alone, stop holding out on me.
HE: Holding out? I don't get you.
SHE: You know what I mean. What really happened last night? What went wrong at the party?
HE: Now wait a minute, Baby. I can't tell you. I wasn't even there.
SHE: After all you promised—and now you're lying to me.
HE: Oh look, Darling. I'd tell you if I could. You know that.
SHE: I thought we'd agreed to be partners, but it looks like this partner doesn't count for anything.
HE: Jean, wait a minute. Let me explain.
SHE: You needn't bother to explain anything, Roger—because I know.
HE: Know what?
SHE: I know you were there because you left your lighter—and here it is!
HE: Oh . . . All right. I'm sorry. But it isn't what you're thinking. Now please relax and I'll tell you everything.

In the next chapter one possible solution to this is offered, and a floor plan and camera shots are derived from the performers' movements.

7.2   Performer movement is applicable to other kinds of programs besides drama.

In a televised lesson, for example, the instructor may move to:

. . . signify the change to a new aspect of his subject. Thus, having finished a demonstration at a wall map, he moves away from the map to introduce a new train of thought.

. . . introduce new visual material. Thus, he moves over to the microscope or to the chalkboard.

. . . emphasize a special point, as by moving closer to the camera.

. . . manipulate visual material, as when operating demonstration equipment.

. . . reflect his state of mind, varying from stationary positions for thoughtful concentration to animated striding as he gets enthusiastic about his subject.

. . . impersonate personages in a story which he cites to illustrate a point about his subject matter.

7.3   Movements by your performers can be induced by providing different locations for different segments of the action.

Example: In staging a panel program, an upper level is provided for the opening statements of the mystery guests before they descend to occupy the seats from which they answer the panelists' questions.

Example: The violin in the guest violinist program (Chapter 2) was placed where the host and guest would have to rise and move to it.

8   Induce visual change by lighting.

Example: The mystery guests in a panel program appear first in silhouette and are then lighted, one after another, as they speak their opening lines.

Example: A couple embrace in shadow. When the girl withdraws from the embrace, her head enters a beam of light, the radiance of which expresses her radiant feeling.

9   Visual changes must be motivated.

There is something annoyingly false about the performer who, while talking to camera, gets out of his chair for no apparent reason, perches on his desk for no apparent reason, then stands up and moves around with no particular place to go. Such arbitrarily induced variety is almost as bad as no movement at all, just as shots which are taken with no motivation but visual variety are almost as bad as no takes at all.

Notice that all of the examples of visual change which have been cited in this chapter have been supported by evident reason. For example, the host and guest have to move because the violin they wish to inspect is not where they are seated. The change from silhouetted to lighted mystery guests is in keeping with the situation that panelists and audience are in the dark concerning the identity of these guests.

9.1   A director can go only so far towards inducing visual change unless the program has been planned to provide for such change.

A performer cannot interact unless there are other program ingredients, animate or inanimate, with which to interact. Nor can there be any great amount of shot variety unless there is more than one visual subject to motivate a change of shots. The director cannot be blamed for failing to inject visual interest into a program during which a single performer does nothing but talk.

9.2   Responsibility for meaningful visual changes begins with the program creator—writer, producer, or whoever he may be.

To give the program a chance of being visually stimulating, he should follow one or more of the following suggestions:
. . . Choose subject matter which inherently involves physical movement: a person doing things instead of merely talking.
. . . Otherwise, involve multiple visual subjects—at least two persons, for example, or one person and various inanimate subjects with which this person interacts—so that visual attention can be shifted from one subject to another.
. . . If possible, develop his program in segments, each of which involves a change of visual subject and a different approach to the program objective. For example, "Planning Your New Home" might be staged by having an architect talk to camera for half an hour. It has a better chance to sustain interest, however, if it is developed in segments such as:

> Hostess shows audience a poor floor plan.
> Hostess and guest architect.
> Hostess introduces couple who are interested in building a new house.
> Couple converse with architect.
> . . . etc.

10   Besides moving your visual subjects, move the mind of your viewer.

When one says that a show moves, he is likely to mean that he has been moved—that his thoughts and perceptions and emotions have been activated and kept active. Good writers and producers know how to move the mind. Good directors should be able to do this with their camerawork.

How can the viewer's mind be moved?

10.1 The mind reaches forward towards the end of something incomplete.

One of the tried and true adages of showbusiness is to "make 'em wait." Suspense and curiosity are mainstays of the successful showman. Your camera can arouse suspense and curiosity by showing a part of the subject before showing the whole, or by panning onto the subject to reveal it by degrees, or by showing it indistinctly first (back to, or in the distance, for instance) before showing it nearer and clearer. Your lighting can do this also, by starting with the subject in silhouette.

The mind reaches forward when an action projects a consequence, and that a further consequence. Consider, for instance, the following shot sequence:

Boy hits ball. (Where did it go?)
Ball smashes window. (What will boy do?)
Boy looks around and starts to run. (Who is coming?)
. . . etc.

In shot editing, it is often effective to cut between an action and reaction or between a deed and its consequence.

10.2 The mind empathizes with the push-and-pull of opposing forces.

Feeling with a force and feeling the desire to resist it set up dynamic tensions in the spectator, which constitute a strong appeal in many kinds of shows and spectator sports. The spectator waits suspensefully for the resolution of the conflict. And when the forces are unbalanced, the lack of equilibrium creates in the spectator a state of unrest with an accompanying urge to see things set aright.

As a director, you can help to build these kinds of excitement by singling out and stressing the opposing forces with your camera. In this connection, review what was said in Chapter 16 about building tension and supporting the degrees of force in the subject matter.

10.3 The mind moves when it makes relations, putting two and two together to draw its own conclusions.

Years ago, silent film makers discovered that the spectator could be given an active part in the creative process by making associations between successive shots. Shot 1 is a closeup of a woman weeping. Shot 2 shows a grave at her feet. That combination yields one kind of association—but if shot 2 shows an onion being peeled in her hands, the spectator forms an entirely different conclusion. This principle of editing is still an effective way to keep your audience actively involved.

The mind can also be activated by being given a chance to realize the bigger picture from a suggestive clue. To suggest is often more effective than to show the whole; and strong dramatic impact often results from finding mental short-cuts in the viewer's imagination so that one activates a whole stream of associations by a single stimulus. Sometimes this stimulus can be completely pictorial. Witness the film sequence in which young English newlyweds dangled clasped hands over a ship's rail, dreaming of the happy life ahead of them in Canada. The scene ended as, straightening up, they withdrew their hands to reveal the label on the life preserver behind which they had been standing: S. S. Titanic.

11   Once you have set the mind in motion, work to preserve its pace.

11.1   Good pace results from economy, from producing a maximum of result with a minimum of means.

In a well paced program each moment is filled with matter that counts. There are no waits, no wasted moments. This holds true in every form of showbusiness. A good entertainer includes just enough to sell his act, sticks to the point, and quits before his audience has had enough. He knows what he is going to do and does it without faltering or fumbling.

In a motion picture the shot of a bell buoy passing tells that the ship has put to sea; thus the film maker makes his point with a minimum of means. He distills and combines, seeking to tell his story with the utmost brevity and power. He begins each scene as close as possible to its high point and cuts to the next scene as soon as the point has been made.

11.2   You, too, can work to eliminate dull and inexpressive moments from your continuity.

Among the causes of such moments are:

. . . performers having to clear off already used demonstration material before bringing new material into view, or having to erase material from a chalkboard before writing new material on it.

. . . performers having to walk unnecessarily far to bring into view the next visual subject, which they have already verbally introduced.

. . . delays in rolling film, or delays in commentary from the studio over silent film because the commentator cannot see the studio monitor.

. . . holding too long on opening theme and titles after the booth announcer has whetted audience desire to see the program.

. . . empty, meaningless visual content traversed during a pan from one subject of interest to another.

. . . late shots, which oblige the performers to mark time until the shots are ready. In this connection, remember what you have already learned about "Keeping Up With the Action."

. . . unnecessarily long dollies-in, when interest has contracted to a portion of the scene before the camera can concentrate the view. To avoid this situation, remember that the wider the lens employed, the less distance the camera will have to travel, and the more quickly it can travel since following focus will be easier. Remember also that a dolly-in from a demonstrator and his product to a closeup of the product will go faster if you compact the wider view as much as possible, for example by keeping the product closer to the demonstrator's face, or by reducing the width of the sponsor's logo behind the demonstrator.

12   Moving the mind requires good timing: the picture must coincide precisely with the action.

Example: In a motion picture which was filmed with a single camera, the turning point came when a man picked up the wrong hat and got a sudden clue to a guilty person's identity by reading the initials on the hat band. For proper shock effect, a closeup of the initials was needed precisely when the act of recognition occurred. Dollying the single camera in for the closeup blurred this important effect.

Example:	DEMONSTRATOR:
CU DEMONSTRATOR LOOKING THROUGH TRANSPAK	(HOLDING PRODUCT UP TO FACE) The next time you go shopping, ask for Transpak.
TILT DOWN TO LEFTOVERS	(LOWERING PRODUCT) Transpak forms a seal to protect your leftovers . . .
PAN TO SANDWICHES	sandwiches for the kids going to school . . .
PAN TO LUNCH	or your husband's lunch.

Here is a typical problem of suiting the picture to the word. The demonstrator must lower her product at precisely the right time to motivate a tilt down to the leftovers, following which the pans to the sandwiches and thence to the husband's lunch box must neatly coincide with the appropriate phrases. A second too late or too soon will be enough to destroy the proper accent.

Example:

IRATE YOUNG LADY: (TURNING FROM THE DESK WHERE THE YOUNG MAN IS SITTING AND STRIDING TOWARDS THE DOOR) . . . And I hope that I never, never see you again—never *ever!* Good-*bye!!!*
(SLAMS THE DOOR)

This is a problem in space-time relationships: the distance from desk to door must be nicely proportioned to the time taken by the young lady to deliver her exit line. The problem begins when you design your floor plan.

12.1   There is a proper moment, too, for every camera take.

No less important than what a picture shows is the time at which it occurs. Good directing requires that you develop your sense of sight, your sense of hearing, and—by no means least—your sense of timing. A book cannot help you much to develop that sense. It is all the more important, therefore, to work on developing it for yourself.

Chapter 19

From Script to Camera Plan

Visual Development of the "He-She" Dialogue

This is the dialogue presented in the preceding chapter, for which you were invited to work out the characters' movements and business. One possible interpretation of this scene will be developed here, starting with the movements and business, then relating these to the cameras and the arrangement of the setting, resulting in a complete plan for visually communicating the action on the screen.

Movement and business

Note the parenthetical directions:

SHE: (CLOSING THE DOOR AFTER SOMEONE WHO HAS JUST LEFT, AND TURNING TO THE YOUNG MAN, WHO STANDS BESIDE HER) All right. Now we're alone, stop holding out on me.

HE: (MOVING AWAY WITH PRETENDED CASUALNESS TO RETRIEVE THE CIGARETTE HE HAS LEFT ON AN ASH TRAY) Holding out? I don't get you.

SHE: (FOLLOWING AFTER HIM TO PRESS THE POINT) You know what I mean. What went wrong at the party?

HE: (TURNING TO FACE HER) Now wait a minute, Baby. I can't tell you. I wasn't even there.

SHE: (MOVING AWAY FROM HIM, WITH INJURED AIR) After all you promised—and now you're lying to me.

HE: (FOLLOWING BEHIND HER) Oh look, Darling. I'd tell
you if I could. You know that.

SHE: (STILL EVADING HIM, AGAIN MOVING AWAY, USING
"HARD TO GET" TACTICS) I thought we'd agreed to be
partners, but it looks like this partner doesn't count for anything.

HE: (FOLLOWING MORE URGENTLY) Jean, wait a minute.
Let me explain.

SHE: (HAVING TAKEN HER PURSE FROM A TABLE, EYES
HIM DIRECTLY) You needn't bother to explain anything,
Roger—(UNFASTENING PURSE)—because I know.

HE: (TRANSFIXED) Know what?

SHE: (REACHING IN PURSE) I know you were there because you
left your lighter—(RAISING IT IN FRONT OF HIS NOSE)
—and here it is!

HE: Oh . . . all right. I'm sorry. But it isn't what you're thinking.
(RESTING A HAND ON HER ARM TO URGE HER
DOWN ONTO SOFA) Now please relax and I'll tell you every-
thing.
(THE NEXT SCENE IS PLAYED SEATED.)

Analyzing the structure of the scene

So that the camera shots may point up the meanings in the scene with
the proper degrees of emphasis, it is necessary to analyze the dramatic construction, asking such questions as the following:

What is the overall action of the scene?

Overcoming the boy's denials with incontrovertible evidence, the girl
forces the boy to an admission.

Is there a climactic pattern to the action?

Yes, the scene develops with rising earnestness and intensity to the
turning point at which the girl produces the lighter.

*Should some speeches be underlined more than others by the visual
treatment?*

Yes, the following are key lines which should make a special impression on the audience:

"What really happened last night? What went wrong at the party?"
(This is the clearest statement of what the girl wants to know.)

"Now wait a minute, Baby. I can't tell you. I wasn't even there." (This
defines the opposing position taken by the boy.)

"I know you were there because you left your lighter—and here it is!"
(This is the turning point, at which the girl wins out.)

The first two speeches delineate the opposing forces which generate
the action; the third speech resolves the action.

The camera shots and their rationale

Camera 1

1 dolly back

SHE: (CLOSING DOOR AND TURNING TO THE YOUNG MAN) All right. Now we're alone, stop holding out on me.

A balanced 2-shot, since so far the forces are equal. The girl commands attention by her turn from the door to the young man. Framing is reasonably loose in order to allow closer shots later for supporting the climax.

HE: (MOVING AWAY) Holding out? I don't get you.

Heading back to his cigarette on an end table, the young man advances towards camera, the camera dollying back with him and leaving the girl in the distance. The movement is made roughly towards the camera, since a lateral movement by the man would probably require losing the girl from the frame. The camera dollies back in order to keep the man's screen size constant, since his line is not sufficiently important to be underscored by enlarging him.

Still on 1

Take 2

SHE: (FOLLOWING) You know what I mean. What really happened last night? What went wrong at the party?

The girl's enlargement as she moves down to him emphasizes the importance of her speech.

HE: (TURNING TO FACE HER) Now wait a minute, Baby. I can't tell you. I wasn't even there.

This speech is reinforced by a take to camera 2, which throws him into the "upstage" position.

2

2

SHE: (MOVING AWAY) After all you promised— and now you're lying to me.

She moves towards camera 2. He follows up to behind her shoulder, saying:

HE: (FOLLOWING BEHIND HER) Oh look, Darling. I'd tell you if I could. You know that.

SHE: (STILL EVADING HIM, MOVING TOWARDS ANOTHER TABLE TO PICK UP HER PURSE) I thought we'd agreed to be partners, but it looks like this partner doesn't count for anything.

2 pan

Camera pans right with her, losing the young man from the frame. Her sidewise cross breaks the pattern of the advancing movements previously employed. There is no need to keep both characters in the shot. Were the shot widened to include them both, they would be too small on the screen. Furthermore, eliminating the young man briefly serves to regenerate interest in him as he re-enters the shot on his next speech.

HE: (FOLLOWING MORE URGENTLY) Jean, wait a minute. Let me explain.

Now they are facing each other directly and in stationary positions which, in contrast to the previous fluid movement, add tension to what is about to occur.

Still on 2

SHE: (HOLDING PURSE, EYEING HIM DIRECTLY) You needn't bother to explain anything, Roger—(UNFASTENING PURSE) because I know.

Since the previous two speeches have been devoted to picking up the purse and the young man's re-entry into the shot, it is this speech during which the stationary confrontation is actually achieved.

HE: (TRANSFIXED) Know what?

The stationary confrontation continues.

SHE: (REACHING IN PURSE) I know you were there because you left your lighter—(RAISING IT)—and here it is!

Take 1

A take to a closer shot, strongly favoring the girl and tight enough to throw considerable attention to the lighter as she raises it in front of his nose, serves to underline the turning point of the scene.

HE: Oh . . . all right. I'm sorry. But it isn't what you're thinking. (URGING HER DOWN ONTO SOFA) Now please relax and I'll tell you everything.

Take 2

The beginning of a new trend of action is marked with a new, looser shot from camera 2.

The floor plan (Figure 19/1)

In devising the floor plan, the first relationship to be established was that between the door and camera 1's first location. Next came the placing of the end table where he had left his cigarette, and the adjacent arm chair was added to justify having an end table in this location. Then camera 2 was located where it could favor the young man on its first take. There remained only to locate the table to which the girl moves to get her purse, and to place the sofa next to this table. The other arm chair was added for set dressing. Still other items would probably need to be included in the room for the same reason.

Fig. 19/1

Camera lenses remain to be selected. For this, you remember, a scaled floor plan needs to be drawn. Perhaps at this point you would like to take over and finish the assignment.

DUST 'N WAX Commercial

The following commercial was written by a student of advertising and turned over to a student of directing to realize on camera:

MOTHER AND DAUGHTER BY COUNTER FINISHING FLOWER ARRANGEMENT	DAUGHTER: The guests are going to think that you're an artist, Mom. The flowers look great.
MOTHER PICKS UP FLOWERS AND CAMERA LEADS MOTHER AND DAUGHTER INTO LIVING ROOM	MOTHER: Why thank you. Let's put them on the coffee table and then get ready for the party. The guests will be here soon.

	DAUGHTER:
MOTHER AND DAUGHTER STEP-PING TO TABLE	Oh Mom look—there are glass stains all over the table.
	MOTHER:
TIGHTER SHOT OF MOTHER AND DAUGHTER FAC-ING EACH OTHER	Well, that's no problem. We can wipe them right away with spray-on DUST 'N WAX.
	ANNOUNCER:
TAKE TO A CU OF DUST 'N WAX	Smart mother, she knows about new DUST 'N WAX, the polish that sprays on for a quick shine . . .
DISSOLVE TO DAUGHTER LOOK-ING AT CAN OF DUST 'N WAX AND MOTHER HOLDING FLOWERS	Spray-on DUST 'N WAX is so quick and easy to use. Anyone can polish furniture with it . . .
MS OF DAUGHTER SHAKING CAN	Just shake the can gently . . .
TIGHTER SHOT OF DAUGHTER SPRAYING WAX ON TABLE	Spray the wax on the furniture . . .
CU OF TABLE BE-ING WIPED	And wipe it off right away. There's no waiting, no rubbing.
	DAUGHTER:
DAUGHTER POINT-ING TO TABLE AND MOTHER HOLDING FLOWERS	Mom, look how it shines. This DUST 'N WAX worked so fast.
	MOTHER:
WIDER SHOT OF MOTHER AND DAUGHTER PLAC-ING FLOWERS ON TABLE	And the shine won't scratch, either.
	ANNOUNCER:
DISSOLVE TO CU OF DUST 'N WAX	So for those last-minute shines on your furniture, get new spray-on DUST 'N WAX today.

The director's analysis of the script

He reviews his general objectives.

The director should focus attention definitely on whatever elements of the scene carry the meaning at each moment of the action. What will appear in the frame? What will be excluded as negative, non-essential, or distracting?

The director's shots should support the degrees of force that are found in the script. Within a given shot, which element should be emphasized as most important? Within a succession of shots, which should make a stronger impression than others? (In a commercial, shots of the product or of what it can accomplish are usually expected to be more forceful than other shots.)

The director is also expected to punctuate his shots to mark and reinforce the divisions of the action or thought—not cutting during a passage that should seem continuous, nor, on the other hand, failing to change his picture statement when the action or thought takes a new turn.

With these objectives in mind, he analyzes the script as follows:

(1) *Mother and daughter talk about the flowers and the party.* This is a shared conversation; therefore, include both persons, and from an angle which will favor them equally. Being merely introductory, the scene should carry little force compared with what is to follow; therefore, a relatively loose shot is appropriate.

(2) *Daughter discovers glass stains on the table.* This is the complication of the plot which is resolved by use of the product; hence it must be more strongly pointed up. The meaning is carried by the daughter and the table; to include the mother will weaken the spectator's concentration on the essential factors. Hence, let the daughter precede the mother towards the table and pan with her into a one-shot. Getting off the mother will also lend impact to her reappearance, which introduces the product.

(3) *Mother suggests DUST 'N WAX.* A cut here will lend impact, saying, "Look, this is new. This is important!" Emphasis should be on the mother. But rather than taking a one-shot, an over-shoulder two-shot will show the new physical relationship between the characters, making it clear that the mother is still in the kitchen area, where she can get the product from a cabinet. To avoid empty space between the figures on the screen, an angle shot is advisable. By showing their different distances from camera, this shot will also promote a feeling of depth on the two-dimensional screen.

(4) *Announcer ratifies mother's recommendation.* Vigorous emphasis on the product demands the most forceful shot yet. Hence a take, and also an abrupt change of shot content and of scale, shooting the can as close as possible and further emphasizing it by putting it in sharp focus against a defocused background.

(5) *Mother brings product to daughter.* It seems better to substitute this action shot for the author's static prescription of "daughter looking at can and mother holding flowers," which does not say much and does not explain how the daughter got the can which she is about to put to use. For the revised action, one can return to the previous over-shoulder shot. As the mother moves forward, she and the can she carries will grow in size and importance. Reaching the table, she can give the can to her daughter in exchange for the bowl of flowers.

(6) *Daughter demonstrates product.* Mother is not important here, so back to an angle which throws the emphasis on her daughter and the table. Since the table waxing is a continuous action, there is no reason to break it up with different shots. But the meaning gradually concentrates and climaxes on the spraying and wiping actions and their result: a polished table surface. This narrowing down can be achieved by a dolly-in.

(7) *Mother and daughter express satisfaction with the result.* A balanced two-shot will reinforce their mutual satisfaction; and the return from angular to symmetrical composition may, through stabilization, promote a feeling of resolution to the outcome of the plot.

(8) *Announcer's tag urges viewers to use product.* The can should be framed as in the previous closeup of it, since it's the same can—before untested, now a proven "hero." But this time, a take to it would be too abrupt, making it seem to be another suddenly occurring incident in the action. This time, mother and daughter have solved their problem, and their resultant satisfaction should linger a while, blending into and thus being associated with the product which has solved their problem. Hence, the product should be introduced by a dissolve.

All of the foregoing considerations (or others equally detailed) pass through the conscientious director's mind, although more swiftly and instinctively than would appear from the written analysis.

The director must now realize his visualization by planning his camera treatment.

Ultimately this results in the floor plan sketched in *Figure 19/2.* Some of the considerations which influenced this plan are as follows:

The setting must be accommodated to certain limitations in the production circumstances.

Fig. 19/2

Directing classes normally have no budgets for scenery and little time for setting and striking it. Hence, the director uses existing studio drapes and, for further backing in the party area, a three-fold screen which is quick to erect and remove. He also uses an existing built-in kitchen, with an island counter where mother and daughter can complete the flower arrangement and a cabinet from which the can of wax can be procured.

The director must check his alternation of cameras.

Thereby he insures that each camera will be available to take the shots expected of it—for example, that camera 1 will be available to take both closeups of the can on the pedestal.

He must work out exact locations for his cameras and for their subjects.

Thereby he insures that each subject will be framed at the correct distance and from the proper angle. For example, camera 1 opens with a shot of mother, daughter, and flower bowl upstage of the counter, then pans with the daughter to the table. The camera distances from counter and table must be such as to permit the exact framing desired, both at the beginning and the end of the pan.

Time for camera deployment must be considered.

The can on the pedestal, which is taken in closeup, must be quite close to camera 1 so that it can be taken on the same lens as used for the previous shot, since there is too little time to chance changing to a different lens and focusing it. To take the second closeup of this can, camera 1 must return very quickly to its original location after having dollied towards the table to look more closely at the polished surface. There must also be time for camera 2 to move between shots from its opening location (aimed towards the kitchen) to its final location (aimed towards the drapes). As things worked out, both cameras were able to make these moves safely, but with little time to spare.

Both video and audio requirements must be kept in mind when selecting furniture.

For the opening tableau, the director specifies a counter away from the wall, since a wall counter would have tended to face the performers away from camera. He specifies a high counter in order to reduce the vertical distance between the flower bowl and the performers' faces, thus permitting a closer shot.

Whereas the writer of the commercial specified a coffee table to be polished, the director chooses a table of normal height. Otherwise, the daughter would have to stoop or kneel to do her polishing while the mother remained standing. Not only would this require a longer shot, making the performers smaller on the screen, but it would also raise the problem of balancing audio levels between mother and daughter, since the daughter would be some distance below the boom microphone, which, to keep out of the picture, would have to remain above the mother's head.

In rehearsal, there must be work with the performers' business.

For example, an abrupt stop and turn to her mother will help to visualize the daughter's dismay when she discovers the glass stains on the table. Business at the table must be timed to the announcer's lines. After the mother has given the can to her daughter and taken the bowl of flowers, she must retire sufficiently to be out of camera 1's shot of the daughter polishing the table.

Finally, the resultant commercial is intended to go like this:

FADE UP 1—Mother, daughter, and bowl upstage of counter

DAUGHTER:
The guests are going to think that you're an artist, Mom. The flowers look great.

PAN WITH DAUGHTER TO TABLE

MOTHER:
(HANDING BOWL TO DAUGHTER, WHO CARRIES IT TO ADJOINING AREA)
Why thank you. Let's put them on the table and then get ready for the party. The guests will be here soon.

DAUGHTER:
(STOPPING AND TURNING) Oh Mom look—there are glass stains all over the table.

TAKE 2—Daughter and table in right foreground, mother in left background, still in kitchen

MOTHER:
Well, that's no problem. (GOING TO CABINET) We can wipe them right away with spray-on DUST 'N WAX.

TAKE 1—CU of can in limbo

ANNOUNCER:
Smart mother, she knows about new DUST 'N WAX, the polish that sprays on for a quick shine . . .

DISSOLVE TO 2—Same as previous shot, with mother advancing to camera left of daughter

(MOTHER BRINGS CAN TO DAUGHTER AND TAKES FLOWERS FROM HER.)
Spray-on DUST 'N WAX is so quick and easy to use. Anyone can polish furniture with it . . .

TAKE 1—Daughter and table top (2 MOVE LEFT)

(DAUGHTER SYNCHRONIZES HER BUSINESS WITH ANNOUNCEMENT.)
Just shake the can gently . . .

DOLLY IN TOWARDS TABLE TOP

Spray the wax on the furniture . . .
And wipe it off right away. There's no waiting, no rubbing.

TAKE 2—Balanced 2-shot, including table top

DAUGHTER:
Mom, look how it shines. This DUST 'N WAX worked so fast.

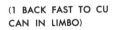

(1 BACK FAST TO CU CAN IN LIMBO)

MOTHER:
(PLACING FLOWERS ON TABLE) And the shine won't scratch, either.

DISSOLVE TO 1—CU can in limbo

ANNOUNCER:
So for those last-minute shines on your furniture, get new spray-on DUST 'N WAX today.

FADE TO BLACK

Chapter 20

Don't Forget Audio

Although this book deals mainly with visual communication, it should not leave the impression that video is more important than audio. To the contrary, much information and enjoyment reaches your audience through its ears.

Some directors become so involved with the look of their program that they ignore what it sounds like. In a way this is understandable. The camera shots tend to demand primary attention because they change more frequently than the sound connections. Furthermore, the director usually has to personally guide the cameras through their paces, whereas for the sound pickup he has the support of the audio engineer.

But this does not excuse the director from knowing what good audio sounds like and how to achieve it. In devising his floor plan, blocking movement, and planning shots, he must reckon with sound as well as picture. During set-up and rehearsal, he must realize when time is needed to remedy an unsatisfactory pickup. As interpreter of the program content, it is for him to prescribe how sound production can best convey that content and to judge with a critical ear whether his standards have been met.

As with the chapters on video, this chapter stresses communication principles rather than technical instruments and, being addressed to beginners, sticks to basic considerations.

Certainly the most basic consideration in sound reproduction is that:

The audience should be able to hear clearly.

This requires that:

(1) The sound is sufficiently distinct. Speakers' voices are not muffled (as when they must pass through a necktie to reach a microphone beneath it). Speech is not overridden by background noise, nor is it distorted by excessive reverberation or by system noise, both of which will be discussed in due course.

(2) The sound is sufficiently loud—and loud enough consistently. It does not keep fading during a speech, or come through loudly when one person is speaking and faintly when the next person speaks. This does not mean that an excited speech should not be heard more loudly than an intimate one. It does mean that you should prevent *unmotivated* volume variations and make even the intimate speech loud enough to hear in your listener's living room. Wherefore this first instruction:

1   Keep the sound loud enough, without unmotivated volume variations.

This requires your attention to three factors: (1) how loud the original sound is, (2) how it reaches the microphone, and (3) how it is regulated by the volume controls. Taking these factors in order now, what can you do about them?

2   Get the performers to speak up.

Television usually requires normal conversational projection, not that of an actor in the theatre projecting to the last row of the second balcony. Nevertheless, speech that is too quiet may require bringing the microphone closer than is feasible or raising the volume control to the possible detriment of sound quality.

When two performers are on the same microphone it is troublesome if one speaks more faintly than the other. Sometimes this can be remedied by placing the microphone closer to the fainter voice. Otherwise, continual adjustments of the volume control will be needed as the speakers alternate, and if the control operator does not know when the alternations are to occur, he may make each adjustment too late.

Since a boom microphone rides above the performer's head, it requires him to literally speak *up* rather than too much downwards towards the notes he may be holding or the properties he may be handling on a table surface.

If the boom must be farther from one speaker than another, you may have to ask the farther speaker to compensate by raising his voice. This situation can occur when one of the persons is seated, hence farther from a boom microphone which must remain above the standing person's head. It can also occur with two standing persons when one is an adult and the other is a child.

The trouble with asking performers to compensate by speaking more loudly at certain times is that, unless they are seasoned performers, they may forget to do so, or else do so unnaturally. Hence you may have to try other remedies. In the situation just cited, for instance, you might ask the adult to stoop down to the child, or place the child on a level which is nearer the adult's head. Thereby you will be fulfilling the next instruction:

3   Keep performers in range of the microphone.

3.1   The microphone should be reasonably close to the speaker and faced as directly as possible towards his mouth.

Pointing the microphone towards the mouth is particularly necessary because most of the microphones used in television, in order to avoid off-stage noises, pick up sound from only one direction, embracing an angle which, for some boom microphones, may be as narrow as $30°$. The farther outside this angle a sound originates, or is directed, the fainter its pickup will be. Hence, for example, care must be given to locating table microphones when seated performers have to turn their heads between various centers of attention—but the problem is always present with microphones however mounted.

Keeping the microphone close enough to a moving performer is most easily solved by using an instrument variously called a neck, chest, or lavalier microphone, which the performer usually wears suspended by a cord around his neck. At the time of writing, many such microphones are connected to the system by cables. These cables can be unsightly in long shots. Performers may move awkwardly with them until they have learned to fasten them at the back of the waist and trail them like a lady's train. When moving around a chair or table, they must remember to return by the same path to avoid becoming wound up. And to avoid entanglement, when several persons are trailing cables they should avoid crossing each others' paths.

More convenient for moving performers is the cableless microphone with a small transmitter which can be concealed on the wearer's person. This is also useful in outdoor locations where untethered movement is required and the terrain is not feasible for stringing cables or deploying booms. At the time of writing, however, transmitter microphone systems of adequate sound quality are still too expensive to have attained the general use to which they may ultimately be put.

For all frankly televised performances, the public has become accustomed to seeing microphones worn by performers and, indeed, may not even be aware of them when they are covered by clothing sufficiently to be unobtrusive. It is difficult to avoid muffling the pickup, however, when the sensitive end of the microphone is covered by a dense fabric. And even when the microphone is exposed, there may be some audio fading when the speaker turns his head.

Keeping the voice within range of the microphone, however, presents more frequent and varied problems when using the microphone boom. The following advice about microphone-performer relationships is all concerned with the use of this boom.

3.2   Keep the boom microphone in mind when working out your floor plan.

When your program requires an extensive playing area, it is advisable to lay in on your floor plan the arcing swath covered by the boom microphone so that you will be sure to keep the performers within range of the microphone. With the boom commonly used at the time of writing, performers cannot move much closer to the boom pivot than 9 feet, nor much farther away from it than 19 feet. To cover additional territory, the three-wheeled perambulator base of the boom can be moved if a man to pull it is available, but except for pulling straight backwards, it is not exactly easy to maneuver. Furthermore, there is a limit with this base to the arc which the boom can traverse without pushing the operator off his platform. In *Figure 20/1* the operator has sufficient room when the microphone is at "B", but at "A" his position is becoming precarious. As things stand in *Figure 20/1,* however, there is no chance of swinging the boom to "A" anyway, because its rear extension will not clear the too-close studio wall.

When relating performers to your setting, as mentioned earlier in this book, anticipate a pickup problem if they must speak when facing a nearby vertical surface, as when writing on a wall-mounted chalkboard or looking out a window. In such circumstances there may not be room to place the microphone far enough in front of their faces.

Fig. 20/1

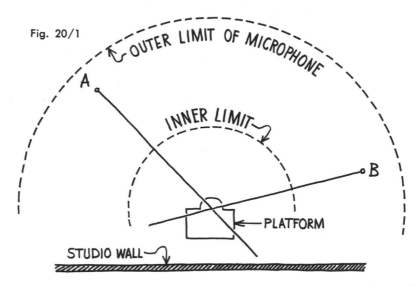

As also noted in the chapters on video, to locate performers close to the walls of the setting is to invite the appearance of boom shadow unless special attention is given to lighting, including the need to obtain a desirable relationship between the direction of the boom and the direction of the key light. If the boom operator has to avoid boom shadow, he may not achieve the microphone position most favorable for sound pickup.

3.3 When blocking action, remember that some performer movements are difficult to follow with the boom.

In *Figure 20/2,* for instance, a performer is speaking while going upstairs. This seemingly simple and direct movement requires the boom operator to simultaneously retract the boom, swing it from left to right, and raise it, while rotating the microphone counterclockwise to keep it facing the speaker.

But it does not take stairs to create difficulties. Suppose that a performer merely faces about. During the time required for the boom operator to react to this occurrence,

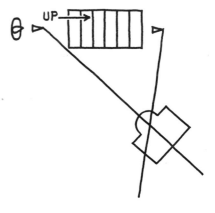

Fig. 20/2

swing the boom over the person's head, and rotate the microphone 180°, a number of words can have faded, sometimes beyond intelligibility. Even more words can be lost should the speaker walk as soon as he has turned. Then, after the microphone has caught up with him, suppose that he unexpectedly sits down. While not as damaging as his previous maneuver, perhaps, his sitting could more than double the distance between his mouth and the microphone until the operator has again caught up with him.

These examples lead to the following suggestions:

(1) When blocking action, question how complicated it may be for the boom operator to follow each of the movements you contemplate.

(2) Test during facilities rehearsal at least the most problematic movements in order to familiarize the boom operator with them and, if necessary, revise them.

(3) During performance, besides calling the camera shots, keep alerting the boom operator to difficult maneuvers before they occur.

(4) When programs are ad libbed or lack facilities rehearsal, keep your prescribed action simple enough for the boom operator to follow. Also, caution your performers against making sudden and pronounced changes in the pace and direction of their movements.

3.4   Audio fading can also occur when speakers are standing still.

For example, when two performers are conversing face to face across a distance of four or five feet, although the boom can remain stationary between them, the microphone will have to reverse 180° with each change of speaker. If these changes are frequent and unexpected, it will take a nimble operator to keep up with them.

When performers are so far apart that the boom has to swing back and forth between them, audio fades can occur unless each speaker keeps silent until the microphone reaches him. But even if the speakers do remember to hold their lines, the cure may be as bad as the complaint, since such pauses, repeated frequently, would make the conversation too halting. Therefore, if the director has but one boom at his disposal, he must either play his talent close together, or have the new speaker move up to the microphone before his lines, or have the current speaker, during his closing words, lead the microphone towards the next speaker.

In televising plays, where characters must often be separated by the requirements of the dramatic action, the problem has occasionally been met by hanging a network of fixed, omnidirectional microphones over the playing area. A more recent solution is to equip every player with a concealed transmitter microphone. Otherwise, two or more booms are used for the pickup. The deployment of these booms must be carefully planned and co-ordinated to avoid their colliding and to prevent audio interference, a disturbance which will be explained later in this chapter.

When the boom operator is covering a group of persons (such as a small studio audience which has been invited to voice comments or to ask questions), he must anticipate who is going to speak next if he is to get the microphone to him in time. One solution is to ask those who desire to speak to raise a hand or stand up, and then wait to be recognized before beginning to talk. The same need for advance identification exists when a "shotgun" microphone is being aimed at individuals in a larger audience.

3.5   The distance between performer and boom microphone is influenced by the height of the camera shots.

The longer the shot, the higher the headroom which usually must be provided to obtain a satisfactory pictorial composition; hence, the higher the microphone must be raised to stay out of the picture, raising with it the likelihood of a poor audio pickup. When very high shots are essential, the boom must give way to some other means of pickup—performer-worn microphones, perhaps, or frankly exposed fixed microphones—or the sound may be pre-recorded so that no pickup at all is required while the cameras are operating. (A fuller discussion of pre-recording appears later in this chapter.)

When the boom microphone is employed, its operator must be alert to vary the height of the boom, raising it before each long shot and lowering it for each closeup which requires the pickup to sound more intimate or closer to the listener. To anticipate each shot, he may find a shot list as useful to him as it is to the cameramen. Lacking this, remember that his knowledge comes from listening to your instructions to the cameramen. Even if Camera 2 is ready for the next shot, your "2, ready for the 3-shot" is also telling the boom operator, "Be ready to raise the microphone," and a "Hold 2" just before "Take 2" may serve as his command of execution. You can also help the boom operator by being sure that a video monitor is stationed where he can see it to check against boom shadow or the microphone itself appearing in the picture.

There is also another person with whom you must cooperate:

4   Cooperate with the audio control operator in his efforts to achieve acceptable volume settings.

The various sound inputs of your program pass through the audio console, where channels are opened and closed and volume adjusted by the audio control operator. Except in the largest stations, he also operates the turntables and audio tape recorders and is responsible for the set-up of microphones in the studio.

4.1 Before set-up time, provide all of the information he needs about your requirements.

He should know the various sources of sound in your program, how the setting will be arranged, where the talent will be stationed and will move within it, and the sequence of events as indicated by your script or rundown. (When preparing the script, by the way, make the audio cues sufficiently prominent for the operator to follow with minimum dependence on your verbal instructions.)

In accordance with his advance information, the operator should be able, before the start of facilities rehearsal, to select the appropriate microphones, install them where needed, and connect them to the channels which will allow the most effective control of their volume. He should also have located the desired starting and stopping places on the tapes and records he is to play and determined the control settings which will transmit them at the proper volume level. Next, he will be ready to set the levels of the performers' microphones.

4.2 As soon as the performers are ready, give the operator an opportunity to set their volume levels.

No matter how loudly the performer speaks, or how much on microphone, his transmitted voice will be too faint if the volume (or "gain") control is set too low. In setting a level, the operator finds the desirable setting for the average or normal degree of loudness delivered by the sound source, a setting which will allow the quieter sounds to still be intelligible and will also permit the louder sounds to be transmitted acceptably. With this setting established, the operator should have a minimum need to ride gain (i.e., to adjust the volume controls) during the performance.

Your part in setting the levels is to ask the performers to run through a sample of their lines or music. When only ordinary conversation is involved, a few random sentences will suffice from each performer; only be sure that the sentences are spoken at the volume to be used in performance. When the program involves music or drama, the operator will need a sample of the loudest and softest sounds that are to occur before he can establish the correct average setting.

4.3   During performance, warn the operator of pronounced changes in volume before they occur.

This is especially necessary when the operator has not listened to a preliminary run-through of the program.

One example should suggest why your warnings are important: Assume that an instrumental band has been playing so loudly that the operator has turned down his volume control in order to keep the sound signal within the permissable range. Suddenly the band stops, and one of the performers begins talking in his ordinary voice over the same microphone which has been picking up the much bigger sound of the band. The reduced setting for the big sound is too low to make the speaker sufficiently audible; hence, part of his words will be missed before the operator has reacted to the change and turned up the control. Had the director readied the operator, this need not have happened.

So far, this chapter has been devoted to just one of the director's responsibilities in the realm of audio: that of insuring that his audience can hear the program with steady and consistent clarity. It is now time to consider another responsibility which, particularly in musical and dramatic programs, may demand a good share of the director's attention—namely:

The sound heard by the audience should seem to be a faithful reproduction of the event being televised.

For example, does the orchestra sound larger than the voice of the persons who introduced it? Can one hear the different instruments in their correct proportions? Is there sufficient distinction between passages marked *piano* and those marked *fortissimo?* Is a voice from the distance fainter than one close to the camera? Does the vocalist's tonal quality seem full and vibrant—or boomy and hollow as if coming out of a barrel?

The purpose of this section is to point out some factors which must be controlled in order to give favorable answers to questions such as those just asked. To start with the last of those questions:

5   Pay attention to audio quality.

The quality or character of a sound is determined by its component frequencies. The range and distribution of those frequencies determine what the sound sounds like—whether like a flute or a steamboat whistle, Mary's voice or Susan's voice—whether thin or full, tinny or harsh, or whatever.

Good reproduction of sound quality depends on (1) preserving the range and distribution of the frequencies in the original sound, and (2) protecting the reproduction from distortion by spurious frequencies.

5.1   The instruments used to transmit sound may alter its frequency pattern.

For example, a voice heard over the telephone does not sound as it does when you hear it directly. A transmitting instrument may alter sound either by failing to reproduce its total range of frequencies or by stressing some frequencies at the expense of others. Thus, a dynamic microphone tends to favor high frequencies, making a tone sound higher, whereas a velocity microphone tends to favor low frequencies, making a tone sound deeper. Models and makes of microphones vary considerably in their frequency response. Consult with your audio engineer to obtain the ones most suitable for your purpose. For music reproduction use the most responsive ones available. When using multiple microphones on the same pickup, select those with similar response characteristics lest the same audio input sound different on each. And when resuming a recording session after an interval during which the equipment has been struck, use either the same microphone or one matching that employed for the previous session.

Sometimes, of course, you may wish to simulate the sound of an instrument which does not transmit a full range of frequencies. To represent the sound of a telephone or loudspeaker, your studio may be equipped with a variable frequency filter, which can cut off high or low frequencies, or both. This may also prove useful for the voices of robots or of things that walk in the night.

In film production, sound which is recorded optically on the film in the camera is of lesser quality than that recorded on magnetically striped film in the camera, or that reproduced by a separate magnetic tape recorder, synchronized with the camera's speed. This latter process, known as double system recording, is advisable for protecting the quality of good music.

5.2   Quality is influenced by the environment in which a sound originates.

Some sound waves from the source pass directly into the microphone; others reach it only after reflecting off surfaces such as the floor and walls. Reflections from distant surfaces, by taking a comparatively long time to return, will produce echo, whereas speedier reflections often enhance the original tone by adding reverberation. Radio and sound recording studios are often designed to provide controlled reverberation for giving a vibrant, "live" quality to voice and music. Television studios are apt to be less reverberant since their walls, being designed to absorb unwanted operational noise, are less reflectant. Even so, you may be concerned with reverberation in the following instances:

The output of a microphone which is close to a reflectant surface sounds different from that of one with much space around it. When using table microphones, therefore, you may need to cover the table top with a sound-deadening material.

The degree of reverberation in a sound pickup should correspond with the supposed location of the program action. If at the seashore, for instance, reverberation would be minimal, whereas in a cave there might likely be echo. To simulate the latter location, your station may have an echo chamber through which the microphone output can be processed.

Different studios, or even sometimes different areas within the same studio, may differ in reverberation characteristics. Remember this and check it out if, for some reason, segments of a sequence which you are recording piecemeal are assigned to different locations.

Sometimes an announcer is established on camera and microphone at a remote site to introduce action which is to occur there; then the rest of his commentary (which will be heard over the action) is recorded at the studio. In this case, there may be a noticeable difference in the reverberation characteristics of the two environments, and also a contrast between the quiet studio and the background sound of the remote location. This latter discrepancy is sometimes disguised by recording "wild" sound at the location and mixing it with the voice recorded at the studio.

5.3 Quality varies with the physical relationship between sound source and microphone.

The distance between sound source and microphone should be such as to minimize the pickup of unwanted sounds. A microphone that is too distant is liable to transmit offstage operational noises. A microphone that is too close to a mouth may put an undue emphasis on breathiness, sibilance, lip smacking, and tongue clacking; and one that is too close to a piano may register the action of the pedals or the rustling of sheet music being turned.

Furthermore, the distance between sound source and microphone also determines what frequencies are picked up from the desired sound. A close microphone transmits less of the reflected sound, and more of the higher and lower frequencies in the direct sound. Such reproduction is said to have "presence," meaning that it contains the full (and presumably satisfying) range which characterizes a sound when it is sufficiently close to the hearer to establish its true quality. By contrast, when the microphone is too distant, the pickup will be thin, roomy, hollow, and lustreless—and if the gain has to be raised to obtain sufficient volume, the pickup will also exhibit proportionately more of the spurious noise which is generated by the electronic system from causes as various as the structure of iron oxide particles on magnetic tape and the flow of electrons in vacuum tubes.

Audio reproduction of a large source such as the sounding board of a grand piano will vary according to which part of the source the microphone is near or is aimed at. Placing the microphone off the tail end of the piano will favor the treble frequencies, whereas placing it off the right end of the keyboard, perpendicular to the direction of the strings, will favor the bass. The pickup will also be influenced by the height and inclination of the microphone, by whether it is raised where it can "see" the strings, or lowered to aim at the underslant of the raised lid, or aimed down to pick up reflections off the floor.

When high fidelity is important, as when good music is being played by competent artists, take special pains with microphone placement. Heed the advice of competent audio specialists. Allow sufficient time for critical listening. Listen for the full range of frequencies in their proper proportions, plus the proper degree of desired reverberation—minus unwanted kinds of reverberation and irrelevant and disturbing factors either in the intended source or from sources which have no business intruding.

5.4 In certain circumstances, good audio quality may require pre-recording.

A string quartet with an international reputation was engaged for a series of programs on national educational television. For a number of reasons its members felt that their music would fall below their high standards if it were recorded during the videotaping sessions: they might be too tired by re-takes to play well; their physical relationship to the microphone and to each other, being partly determined by shot requirements, was not the one to which they were accustomed; and the studio was not sufficiently reverberant to produce the desired vibrancy of tone. So they made audio tapes of their performances in their own sound studio. During camera sessions at the television station, the studio microphones were cut, and their own audio tapes, besides being fed to the video tape recorder, were played to them through the studio loudspeaker so that they could synchronize with them as they played for the cameras. Thus, their standards of audio quality were upheld by pre-recording.

Pre-recording is also used in song and dance shows, particularly for production numbers. Obviously, a singer who is moving and turning rapidly in various directions is very difficult to keep on microphone. Furthermore, it is a rare artist who can undergo such exertions and still produce commendable vocal quality. And in spectacles which require wide shots, boom microphones may have to be raised so high that good audio pickup is next to impossible. All such difficulties can be circumvented by pre-recording.

Brief mention should also be made of post-recording. This has its uses in filming at remote locations where satisfactory audio is difficult to attain either because microphones cannot be suitably placed or because unwanted sounds (such as automobile and airplane traffic noises) cannot be avoided. Although, to produce visible lip movements, the performers go through the dialogue during the filming, the sound actually used on the program is recorded later at the studio. There, the filmed action may be projected over and over while the performers work to synchronize their utterance with the lip movements on the screen.

5.5   Quality is difficult to achieve when the transmitted sound is desired to be very quiet or extremely loud.

Mention has already been made of the spurious noise which is generated by the reproducing system. The fainter the program sound is desired to be, the more it comes into competition with this system noise, producing what is called an unfavorable signal-to-noise ratio.

On the other hand, extremely loud sounds are liable to what is called amplitude distortion. For example, when recording sound on audio tape, the maximum volume which you can record with good fidelity will depend on the power output of your amplifier. Normally, the amplifier's power output will increase proportionately to increases in the signal put into it—but if the input signal is increased in volume (i.e. amplitude) to the point where the amplifier is putting out as much power as it possibly can, further increases will produce the distortion.

The audio control operator assigned to your program at the studio also has to guard against distortion by keeping the needle on his VU meter from peaking too far into the red region of the scale. If he allows sounds to peak at more than +1 or +2 volume units, they will be distorted by automatic limiters and compressors which prevent the transmitter from overloading.

This introduces another kind of problem in achieving an acceptable reproduction of the program audio content. Besides preserving the quality of the original sound, you must preserve the distinctions in its volume variations.

6 Work, within the conditions of the medium, to transmit the relative degrees of loudness in a sequence of sound.

Thus, you should try to insure that the finale of the *1812 Overture* will sound appreciably louder than the announcement which follows it—and that actors' whispers will be softer and their shouts louder than their normal conversation—and that the performance of Ravel's *Bolero* will be heard as one steady crescendo from a faint beginning to an almost overwhelming ending.

6.1 But do not expect to transmit as much volume contrast as the program may contain.

There may actually be an enormous difference in volume between a speaking voice and the finale of the *1812 Overture* as heard in the concert hall. But the sound systems of home television receivers are not capable of reproducing this range—nor would most members of your audience enjoy the full impact of a 100-piece orchestra in their living rooms. Also, they do not enjoy sudden, great increases in volume, as might naturally occur when a verbal introduction is followed by the brassy opening of a band selection. These are some of the reasons why broadcast music is not transmitted at a level greatly louder than that of speech.

Another reason for restricted volume range was cited a few paragraphs ago: soft sounds run into competition with signal noise, and loud sounds are liable to amplitude distortion. Therefore, there are audio control operators who resist letting the needle on their VU meter drop below 40% modulation or shoot beyond 100% into the red region.

The restricted range of the system can be a problem when one is trying to reproduce music or dramatic speeches which contain passages much softer or louder than the 40 to 100% bracket allows. Keeping the needle within the bracket compresses the sound at both ends, eradicating all distinctions within the softer passages on the one hand and within the louder passages on the other.

6.2 When faced with this problem of compression, there are some things you can do to improve the situation.

In some ways you can try to keep the performance within the transmittable volume range. For example, you can avoid casting in an announcer's role the person who habitually blasts out the beginning of sentences or explodes consonants, driving the needle into the red at every other word. And

when directing angry dramatic scenes, you can try to tone down the shouting, working with your actors to produce the illusion of extreme loudness
by more projection and less lung power. When working with a band, you
can sometimes get the musicians to hold back their peaks a little. But with
concert and recital music, where every variation in volume has been introduced for a calculated esthetic effect, your best course is to leave the performance unaltered and work with your audio engineer to reproduce it as
faithfully as possible.

If your engineer is a 40 to 100 man, try to get him to give his needle a
little more latitude. It has been known to peak at $+1$ and $+2$ volume units
without causing serious distortion, and for the softest notes, it can drop at
least briefly well below 40, provided that it stays moving.

Let your audio control operator hear the entire composition in advance of performance. Especially when music is concerned, an audio rehearsal is just as important as camera rehearsal, and maybe more so. Only
by having heard the music will the operator know what volume variations
have to be distinguished, and when they occur.

Thus forewarned, he should be able to make compensating adjustments when the music exceeds tolerable range. Knowing where a maximum
peak occurs, he can imperceptibly reduce the volume for half a minute or so
before the peak is due, thus giving it some more latitude in which to rise.
Similarly, he can gradually sneak up his gain before a very faint passage is
due. Thus, he can fit more into the audio suitcase, so to speak, than the
suitcase was built to contain.

Correct reproduction of volume levels requires both an ear to the program sound on the audio monitor and an eye to the signal strength indicated
on the VU meter. Without that meter, the engineer might have the volume
on the monitor turned up enough to hear the soft sounds acceptably, yet
actually be feeding too weak a signal. Remember that the monitor does not
indicate the signal strength. If it happens to be turned down, you might be
tempted to complain that the transmitted sound is not loud enough when a
glance at the meter would show that it is.

That the signal is peaking satisfactorily, however, does not really reveal how the program sounds to your audience. This can be estimated only
by listening. Therefore, the good director will discourage unnecessary chat-
ter in the control room so that he and the engineer can keep their ears on
the audio content.

These ears will be needed to judge not only volume variations, but also
the balance between various sound sources.

7   Multiple sound inputs in a given sequence should be balanced to achieve a natural or intended proportion between their respective volume levels.

7.1   Balance can depend on three factors:

(1) It is affected by the distance between the sound sources and the microphone. For example, when two speakers are on the same microphone, the microphone is placed closer to the one with the weaker voice.

(2) When several microphone channels are used for the same pickup, balance depends on the relative volume settings of these channels. For example, if the two speakers just mentioned are on separate microphone channels, that for the weaker voice will be given a higher setting than the other channel. (Once this balance has been established, it can be kept intact by patching the channels into a submaster so that, instead of riding gain on them separately, their combined output can be adjusted by a single control.)

(3) Remember that, in the first place, the desired balance may already have been established by the performers themselves. Musical groups, for example, may work long and hard to achieve a desired ratio of sound between their component sections. Hence this caution:

7.2   Take care lest you destroy the auditory balance of a musical group by rearranging it in the interests of pictorial composition.

Instrumentalists and the members of vocal choruses become accustomed to established physical arrangements wherein they can regulate their own volume according to what they hear from their colleagues. Likewise, their conductor is accustomed to hear certain sounds coming from certain established directions. Rearranging the parts of an ensemble, therefore, should not be undertaken without its members' consent.

Incidentally, not only balance but also coordination between musicians may be injured if you rearrange them without prior consultation. For example, double pianists may be accustomed to face each other in order to coordinate their playing by nods and eye signals or observation of each other's movements. To place them side by side or back to back may hamper their musicianship.

7.3   Microphone-performer relationships are important when televising bands and orchestras.

It is advisable to keep the more strident and percussive instruments farther from the microphone: thus, reeds in front, brass behind them, and drums in the rear. The piano is usually at one side so that the pianist can see clearly for purposes of accompaniment.

How many microphones should be used to pick up a large ensemble? On this question there are two conflicting theories. One is to avoid any interference with the balance as established by the conductor. This calls for a single microphone out front where it will pick up the aggregate sound much as it reaches the conductor's ears.

Opponents of this theory point out that when instruments (particularly soft-toned ones such as cellos or flutes) are heard in small combinations or solo passages, they may sound thin and faint, lacking presence because of their distance from the microphone. Also, the single microphone cannot always be placed where it will pick up the balance between sections as the conductor hears it. Therefore, these critics advocate at least additional microphones to reinforce the solo instruments; and beyond this, some prefer to cover each section with a separate microphone channel, balancing these channels at the audio console. To avoid upsetting this balance, once achieved, the channels can be controlled by a single submaster, with the possible exception of those covering certain featured instruments, which may need to be controlled separately in order to make them stand out sufficiently against their accompaniment.

7.4   In balancing, protect an important sound source from being dominated by other sources.

For example, a vocal or instrumental solo should stand out against its accompaniment. To this end one can sometimes succeed in getting the accompaniment to be played more softly; otherwise, one must resort to other solutions.

Figure 20/3 shows a common arrangement for a soloist with piano accompaniment. The two sound sources are picked up on separate microphone channels so that their volumes can be adjusted independently. Each microphone is pointed towards its own sound source, with a dead side towards the other source.

Fig. 20/3

In *Figure 20/4,* the pianist himself is singing or talking as he plays, with a single microphone directed towards his mouth. The microphone should be so mounted that it can be reasonably close to the mouth. An over-head boom may serve if it can be dipped low

Fig. 20/4

enough without appearing in the picture. When there is no objection to revealing the microphone, a lavalier may suffice, but better sound can probably be obtained by using a stand-mounted microphone with superior response characteristics.

When a soloist performs in front of an orchestra, his microphone should be separately controlled. It should also be placed so that it does not pick up the orchestra as strongly as it does his voice. If he can face at right angles to the orchestra, the orchestra will be on the dead side of his microphone, but if he must stand in front of the musicians, facing the same way they do, his microphone will be pointed towards them as well as him. In this situation, it helps to bring the soloist as far forward as possible and as close to the microphone as his technique of performance will allow.

7.5   Balancing should take account of audio perspective.

The voice of a distant person should not sound the same as that of a person in the foreground of the picture. Not only should it be fainter, but it should also lack some of the high and low frequencies which are heard in a nearby voice. The easiest way to achieve the effect is to keep the microphone farther away from the distant speaker than the nearby one.

Two major considerations in sound reproduction have now been covered: The audience should be able to hear clearly; and what it hears should seem to be a faithful reproduction of the event being televised. Next, you are being asked to consider what the audience should *not* hear.

The audience should be protected from auditory disturbances.

This rule will serve to introduce a blacklist of things to avoid in audio production either because they impair intelligibility, distract attention, offend sensibility, misrepresent the subject matter, or disrupt the unity of the production.

8   The blacklist can start with some things which have already been discussed, including:

. . . sound which is unintelligible, either because it is too faint or too indistinct.

. . . unmotivated fading.

. . . sound of poor quality, due to insufficient frequency response, or the wrong amount of reverberation, or amplitude distortion, or an unfavorable signal-to-noise ratio.

. . . extreme, abrupt changes in volume level, which may oblige the listener to either turn up or turn down the volume control on his set.

. . . pauses while the microphone is moving from one sound source to another.

. . . volume that is inconsistent with the natural loudness of the source, or with its visible distance from the observer, or with its intended importance relative to other attendant sources.

. . . sound quality that is inconsistent with the auditory characteristics of the assumed environment.

. . . inexpert production of sound by the performers, insofar as the director may occasion this by requiring them to perform under unfavorable circumstances, or may unduly emphasize it, as by tolerating a microphone that is too close.

. . . the presence of irrelevant sound—offstage noise, piano pedal action, etc.

Although this is already a formidable list, still other causes of disturbance should be added to it. Some of these will fit into categories already established, but nevertheless deserve to be singled out for special emphasis. In addition to the foregoing, therefore:

9   Anticipate and prevent, or be alert for and prevent:

9.1   Distracting noises made by performers:

Paper rustling, dish rattling, pencil tapping, etc., carried on too close to a microphone, usually either by performers seated in front of a table microphone or holding things too near a lavalier microphone.

The clunking of lavalier microphones against buttons and tie clips or the edges of desk and counter tops.

9.2   Wind noise:

Indoors, this can be created by too rapid a swing of the microphone boom. Outdoors, your audio engineer should select a type of microphone with minimum sensitivity to wind, and may also need to equip it with a wind-shielding cover.

9.3   Camera blower noise:

This is picked up when a camera with its blower operating comes too near an open microphone. Listen for it on dollies-in close to a performer.

9.4   "Wow":

This word describes the sound of a phonograph record or of a film sound track which is fed into the program before attaining its proper speed. Your cues for film and recorded sound should be delivered early enough to allow whatever time the relevant mechanisms need to attain this speed. Also, because of the delay in attaining speed, it is advisable when picture and recorded theme are to be faded in together (as at the beginning of a program) to cue music before picture, e.g.: "Music, fade up 6."

9.5   "Out of sync":

Recorded sound and picture fail to synchronize with each other, as when the words uttered by performers on a film do not correspond with their lip movements.

9.6   Microphone interaction:

An effect resembling echo sometimes results from a time delay when two microphones are used for the same pickup, one picking up the sound immediately, the other after it has reflected. A filtered effect (as if some of the frequencies have been filtered out) may be heard when two microphones are close together, as when lavaliers or table microphones are picking up persons who are next to each other. This can be prevented by riding down the gain of one microphone while the other is in use.

9.7   Feedback:

Feedback occurs when part of the output of a system returns to its input. In audio production, this is liable to occur when program sound is fed through a loudspeaker into a studio with an open microphone, either to let an audience hear the program or to let performers hear a recorded musical accompaniment. To prevent the excruciating howl which can result from this signal interference, considerable attention may be needed to adjusting the volume of the loudspeaker and to the relative positioning of loudspeaker and open microphones.

9.8   Various errors by the audio control operator:

A sound cue is delayed or missed altogether. The wrong microphone is opened. A microphone is left open when it should have been cut, thus conveying information which the audience is not intended to hear.

Such errors often result from a failure of communication between the director and the operator, particularly when there has been no audio rehearsal and when the operator's written instructions (as on the script or rundown) are deficient, or not sufficiently prominent, or not clear.

10   Two errors which are non-technical in nature also deserve inclusion in a list of auditory annoyances:

10.1   The program lacks a sense of auditory completion.

Specifically, this refers to the closing musical theme which is interrupted in progress as a program fades to black. To give the ear as well as the eye a sense of finality, the director should see that his operator backtimes the recording. For example, knowing that the program is to end at 29:30, and having determined that the track on which the closing theme is recorded lasts one minute and thirty seconds, the operator will start playing the track at 29:00 minus 1:30, or in other words at 28:00. The theme does not have to be heard when the track is started, since the operator can keep the volume faded down until the director cues music.

10.2   Recorded music and program content do not harmonize in character.

A particular example is the bombastic opening theme which precedes comparatively sedate content.

This completes the blacklist—and also those suggestions about audio production which fall within the limits of a book for beginning directors. There is much more for you to learn about the subject than has been presented here. You should become familiar with many kinds of music which you can draw upon for themes and establishing background moods. You will want to experiment with the use of music and sound effects to create mood, atmosphere, and locale, and to tie assorted segments together in the interest of continuity. To prepare yourself for directing music programs, you should learn all you can about instruments and the structure of music. As a director of drama, you will need to cast your actors with an ear to vocal contrast and their capacities for oral expression; you must be able to help them express the meanings of the script by nuances of inflection, tone, and volume, by emphasis and underemphasis, and by changes of vocal pace. And for general purposes you will want to seek further technical knowledge in books and articles on audio production, not only for television, but also for the related media of radio, phonograph records, audio tapes, and motion pictures.

In the meantime, keep in mind this summary advice:

When the cast of your program contains artists who express themselves in sound, consult with them about what they are trying to achieve and how they think you can help them to achieve it.

Rely on your audio technicians; orient them to your requirements; and provide them with sufficient opportunity to achieve those requirements.

Remember that the best arrangement for picture may not be the best one for sound.

Besides looking, keep listening. Don't forget audio!

Chapter 21

The Three "E's"

This book began by reminding you that the television director is an interpreter, charged with conveying faithfully the meanings of whatever action passes through his microphones and cameras. To help you become a good interpreter, you have been furnished with many principles—so many, perhaps, that you may find it difficult to tie them all together. If so, it may help you to realize that, underlying all these principles, there are essentially three important objectives:

1   Like every other communicator, you must make your communication:

Evident — clear to the vision and understanding.
Engrossing—fully occupying the mind and attention.
Effective—producing the intended effect.
These three "E's" should govern every program you do and every shot you take.

2   Your program material will be evident when:

. . . the viewer recognizes what he sees on the screen.
. . . he is oriented to the relative locations of the visual elements in the scene.

. . . he can relate these visual elements to derive the intended meaning from them.

. . . he can relate the pictures in time sequence to derive the intended meaning from them.

. . . he realizes whether each new shot is a continuation of what has been happening or is the beginning of a new train of action.

. . . he discerns the pattern of the subject matter and the units which make up that pattern.

. . . he senses the relative importance of each ingredient.

3 Your program material will be engrossing when:

. . . the viewer's attention is kept stimulated by new experiences.

. . . his mind is kept reaching forward to take in what is coming next.

. . . his concentration is protected from distractions, irrelevancies, and obscurities.

. . . he is kept from being frustrated by not seeing what he wants to see when he wants to see it.

. . . he is stimulated to some engaging activity, e.g.:

> The tensing and releasing of his emotional energy,
> The mental association of pieces of information,
> The sensing of forces in conflict,
> The urge to attain a goal,
> The urge to set things aright,
> Or a motor activity, such as moving in time to rhythmic stimuli.

4 Your program material will be effective when:

. . . the viewer responds to it in the manner intended.

. . . he learns—or is entertained—or is persuaded to some action, whether writing his Congressman or buying a commercial product.

. . . he feels the mood of the love scene, the suspense when the bases are loaded, the danger faced by the circus aerialist. He admires the dexterity of the trumpeter and the coordination of the orchestra.

. . . he notices and reacts as it was hoped he would to every stimulus which the director exposes to him.

5 You can define your job in terms of stimulus and response.

A group of directors at a professional meeting were once amused to hear a behavioral psychologist define their role as "management and control of the stimulus field." On second thought, however, they understood—and so should you.

Think of each picture you show as a stimulus, designed and controlled by you to produce in your viewer a calculated response.

It follows that, within each picture, the viewer's attention should be focused on what the psychologist would call "relevant cues," i.e., those ingredients which will give your viewer an understanding of what is going on and the reaction to it which you expect of him at that moment.

More colloquially, you want him to get the point. So you show him what will make him get that point. This is where Part One started, and also where it ends.

Part Two: ACCESSORY APTITUDES

Part One is solely concerned with principles of communication. It has aimed to develop an aptitude which, beyond all else, it is important for a director to cultivate: that of finding the meaning in the action to be televised and then devising pictures which will communicate that meaning.

But there are other aptitudes which the director must cultivate as accessories to this major one in order to realize the pictures he has visualized. To have his pictures properly staged and lighted, he should be able to make floor plans. To have the right shots readied and taken at the proper moment, he needs to develop his skill in calling shots. And to coordinate all of the activity which goes into preparing and executing the production of his pictures, he must be a model of efficiency.

Such a bearing do these aptitudes have on the director's ability to realize his objectives that it seemed unwise to omit them simply because they did not fit smoothly among the chapters on communication principles. Therefore, they have been retained, but placed in their own separate part. Thus segregated, they may be assigned in any order, if the instructor desires, for reading concurrently with Part One. And without disturbing the continuity of Part One, any chapter in Part Two may be ignored by the reader who considers himself already proficient at the aptitude it discusses.

Chapter 22

Making Floor Plans

1 Floor plans serve two purposes:

(1) They allow you to work out the location of scenic elements, performers, and cameras well in advance of camera sessions, when time is too precious for random experimentation. By experimenting on paper, you can try out many solutions until you have found the best one. By drawing the plan with accurate measurements, you can ascertain in advance that your scheme will work.

(2) This accurate drawing will furnish necessary information to the technicians who are to erect and light your settings, install microphones, and set cameras in their opening positions.

To help you devise your own floor plans, you are going to be shown some simple plans which have been used for staging student production exercises. The first of these (*Figure 22/1*) is for *News and Weather Briefs*.

2 The plans uses symbols and labels.

The triangles with rounded corners indicate pedestal cameras. The long dash lines show the angles of view included by the principal camera shots, the numbers within or near these angles designating the focal length of the lenses to be used for these shots. Other symbols locate the boom

Fig. 22/1

microphone, stands for holding graphic materials, furniture, background, a studio monitor to be watched by the newsman, and even the key locations (a, b, and c) to be occupied by the newsman, which will be helpful information for the persons who will light the show.

Examples of other symbols used in floor plans are shown in *Figure 22/2*. Before making plans at the studio where you work, find out whether there are special symbols used there. Also learn the names by which particular pieces of furniture and scenery are identified there, since labels such as "A-frame," "blonde desk," and "Sampson weathermap" will indicate the specific items you have in mind.

Fig. 22/2

3 The plan is drawn to scale.

Objects on the plan are outlined as if someone had traced around them while they were occupying their proper positions on the studio floor. Since it would obviously be impractical to draw these outlines at their actual size, the plan is drawn to some convenient reduced scale. Every foot of actual size is reproduced by some smaller unit of measurement, large enough to show necessary details yet small enough to fit the paper available. For this unit directors often use a quarter-inch. To fit the pages of this book, however, the scale (as you can read on the plan) is $\frac{1}{8}'' = 1'0''$. This means that every eighth-inch on the drawing represents one foot at actual size. Thus, the desk outline measures $\frac{1}{4}''$ by $\frac{1}{2}''$, which is equivalent to 2 eighth-inches by 4 eighth-inches, showing that the actual size of the desk is 2 feet by 4 feet.

You can save time in laying out floor plans by carrying commonly used dimensions in your head. For example, an interior door opening is often 2'6'' wide, a straight chair is about 18'' square, and a person's shoulders span approximately 18''. If you know that the sides of the base of your camera pedestal measure 39'', you will plan enough space between the table and the sofa for the camera to dolly between them. You can locate your boom microphone properly if you remember that its extension ranges from just over 7' to 17' and that the rear end of the boom extends 5'6''. (The dimensions just cited are not necessarily those of the equipment you may be using.)

Draw to scale not only the scenic objects, but also the distances between them. Only when all relationships have been scaled can you be reasonably sure that the shots you intend are possible and that the scene will be set as you intend it.

4   Lens angles can be tested on the floor plan.

When you have scaled the distance of your camera from a given subject on the floor plan, you can test how much of the subject will be included by various lens angles. As you should already know, the angle of view embraced by a lens depends on its focal length and on the diameter of the face of the pickup tube in the camera being used. Thus, the angle of a 2'' (50mm) lens used on a 3'' image orthicon is 35°, but on a 1'' vidicon only 13-$\frac{1}{2}$°. Some of the angles you may use are as follows:

For 1" Vidicons	*For 3" Image Orthicons*
$\frac{1}{2}'' - 54°$	35mm − 50°
$1'' - 27°$	50mm − 34°
$2'' - 13\frac{1}{2}°$	90mm − 20°
$3'' - 9°$	135mm − 12$\frac{1}{2}$°
$6'' - 4\frac{1}{2}°$	8$\frac{1}{2}$'' − 8°

There are various guides for drawing these angles on your floor plan. With a little ingenuity you can make a device with two straight edges which are pivoted and calibrated to open up (like scissors blades) to the desired angle. Or, with the aid of a protractor, you can draw each separate angle on cardboard, or better, on transparent plastic, and then cut it out, retaining either the cut-out piece or the remaining "jaw." Or, as in *Figure 22/3,* you can simply draw a clump of angles on a sheet of paper which you can slide around under your plan. This requires drawing your plan on paper which is sufficiently translucent so that you can see the angles through it.

Fig. 22/3

The angles in *Figure 22/3* are horizontal angles, which can be used to determine what width of field you will have at a given distance from the lens. The height of the field will be three quarters of the width. This fact was used to establish the proper distance of camera 2 from the newsman's swivel chair on the plan (*Figure 22/1*) (see page 211) for *News and Weather Briefs.*

The first things the director drew on this plan were the swivel chair and the desk in front of it. Then, knowing that he would be using a 3″ image orthicon, and choosing a 90mm lens for the shot, he laid the 20° horizontal angle for that lens underneath the plan, adjusting it until the width which it framed where the seated newsman's shoulders would be measured approximately 32″. The height of the field at this point would be three quarters of 32″, or 24″. This would be sufficient to include some headroom and a little of the desk top. So the angle was traced onto the plan in that position. As you can see by measuring the plan, this placed the front of camera 2 about 8′ from the back of the newsman's chair.

5   The floor plan is derived from the script.

The locations of virtually all the other elements in the set-up were derived from the calculations just described. But to see how these other elements fit in, you will need to read the script for the program, for the floor plan is derived from the script and is devised to carry out the intentions of the script.

That this script is student-written and reflects an undergraduate's sense of humor makes it no less useful as a basis for floor planning.

Numbers in parentheses along the left margin indicate which camera, 1 or 2, the director plans to assign to a shot. In the audio column, the time for beginning each shot has been indicated by the symbol: (X).

(2) CARD: Horse and buggy	*MUSIC: THEME UP & UNDER (OUT AFTER BOOTH ANNOUNCEMENT)*
(1) CARD: News and Weather Briefs	BOOTH ANNCR: The National Association of Local Livery Stables brings you (X) News and Weather Briefs, reported by Horace Trotter. (X)
(2) DISS TO: MS NEWSMAN AT DESK	TROTR: (AT DESK) AD LIB OPENING NEWS STORY, ENDING: . . . And now for the news in pictures. READ BRIEFS ON:
(1) PIC: Man in apron	MAN IN APRON
(2) PIC: Shotputter	SHOTPUTTER
(1) PIC: Spaghetti baby	SPAGHETTI BABY
(2) MS NEWSMAN PAN HIM TO MAP	(X) And that's the news. (RISE & MOVE TO MAP.) Now for the
(1) CU WESTERN HALF OF MAP PAN TO EASTERN HALF	weather from coast to coast. (X) In the West, sun and blue skies from Frisco to Fargo . . . but in the East, tornadoes, typhoons, and thunder showers. (MOVING TO-
(2) NEWSMAN, MOVING TOWARDS CAMERA	WARDS CAMERA) (X) That's the national picture. Now here's the
(1) CU TOP WEATHER BOX (Weather) TILT DOWN (Temperature) TILT DOWN (Pollen)	BOOTH ANNCR: local prediction . . . (X) Today's forecast for this vicinity: cloudy with clearing skies towards evening . . . Maximum temperature 57, minimum temperature 48 . . . Pol-
(2) MCU NEWSMAN	len count six thousand, two hundred and two. (X)
	MUSIC: THEME IN UNDER
	TROTR: Before we say goodbye, here's a closing thought from our sponsor.
(1) CARD: Sponsor ID	BOOTH ANNCR: (X) When you're thinking of rid-
(2) CARD: Horse and buggy	ing, remember: (X) a horse stands head and shoulders above any car on the market!
	MUSIC: UP TO TIME

6 How the director devised the floor plan:

The studio cameras take all the graphics in the program, those on stands outside the playing area as well as the weather map within it. Where graphics follow one another, the director preferred, for the sake of clean transitions between them, to show them on alternate cameras rather than flipping through a sequence of them on a single stand. Early in his considerations, therefore, he tentatively marked the camera numbers on his script to test whether the specified shots would alternate properly between the cameras. For example, the "horse and buggy" card is used twice; would it come up both times on the same camera? Fortunately it did. Fortunately also, all shots of the newsman could be taken by the same camera, thereby allowing the audience a consistent view of him and considerably simplifying the problem of camera placement, since only one camera need be located where it could cover him effectively. It's a blessing when the scriptwriter, as in this case, has been educated to the director's problems.

6.1 In devising his plan, the director first considered the newsman's actions.

It is usually wise to begin by working out, at least tentatively, the performers' actions before deciding too firmly about the camera locations, since these actions, after all, are the subject of the program and the cameras are only the reproducers thereof. In the interests of effective reproduction, the actions may be modified to accommodate the cameras, but not at the expense of becoming less animated and less convincing.

As shown by the script, the action in *News and Weather Briefs* is simple: the performer delivers the news while seated behind his desk, then rises and walks to the weather map, then approaches camera for his closing statements.

You have already seen how the shot of the desk was set up. There seemed to be no reason why the rest of the action could not be taken from the same camera location. In a show which moves as fast as this one, and is also to be shot by student cameramen, unnecessary camera deployment may entail being late for a shot or off position for it. Therefore, the director located the weather map where it and the newsman standing beside it could be taken without moving camera 2. Since this shot required wider framing than the shot at the desk, the map was located farther from camera than the desk. To keep the map from showing during the presentation of the news, it was placed outside the desk shot, but not so far outside that the newsman would not have time to reach it during his brief line, "Now for the weather from coast to coast."

Having fixed the location of the map, the director could now locate camera 1 for its closeup of the map. To avoid perspective distortion, this shot should be perpendicular to the map. To remain outside of camera 2's shots, camera 1 must be on the opposite side of the desk from the map, but not so distant that it cannot get a close shot of a section of the map with at least an 8–½ " lens.

No problem is caused by camera 2's last shot of the newsman. The newsman is to approach camera for this, moving away from the map to signify that the weather reporting has ended. For informality, the director has him walk up to one end of the desk and perch on it. Giving him this point of reference also keeps him from ending up too close to camera.

6.2 *Now it is possible to locate the stands on which the title cards and news pictures will be displayed.*

Here the primary consideration is speed—speed for the camera to move between an easel and its other shots. To avoid unnecessary delay for changing and focusing lenses, the easels are placed where the graphics they hold can be framed on the same lens used for shots of the performer. To minimize the distance which the camera must pan when getting on and off the graphics, the easel for camera 2 was situated just outside of that camera's shot of the map.

For camera 1 there were required both an easel (for three titles and pictures) and an "A-frame" on which to mount the "weather boxes." In locating these stands, a necessary consideration was available labor. Besides the floor manager, there was only one floorman. He could be used for changing the graphics on camera 2's easel. Those on camera 1's easel would have to be changed by the floor manager, who would also have to cue the newsman from a position close to the camera which the newsman would be addressing. Since a picture change occurs almost coincident with the newsman's opening cue, it seemed necessary to locate camera 1's easel where the floor manager could stand between it and camera 2.

6.3 *The plan also locates the microphone boom platform and suggests a direction for the key light.*

Sometimes this information is left for the technicians to decide. Nevertheless, in devising his plan, the director must be sure that any boom which he intends to use can pick up the sound without interfering with his cameras' vision and movements, and also that good lighting is feasible.

Much television lighting operates on the premise that the illumination of a scene should seem to be coming from a principal direction. The light moving from this direction, called the key light, is usually originated by spotlights, and spotlight beams can cause troublesome shadows. By specifying that these beams travel parallel to the weather map instead of towards it, the director aims to keep off that map shadows of the newsman and of the microphone boom.

The direction of the boom also has an effect on shadows. If it is aligned parallel to the key light, a vertical shadow of it may be caught on the performer or his background. When perpendicular to the key light, however, the boom produces a horizontal shadow, which is easier to keep off camera and may be eliminated altogether by lowering a "top barn door" on the instrument which emits the light. Hence, the floor plan for *News and Weather Briefs* provides that the boom take this perpendicular direction.

It is easier to keep unwanted shadows off backgrounds if the backgrounds are kept at some distance behind the performers. This also facilitates backlighting the performers and enables one to control the brightness of backgrounds by lighting them independently of the playing area. For these reasons, the director plotted to keep his newsman well in front of the cyclorama. He also insured that the weather map would not obstruct backlighting aimed on the performer.

One final element specified on the plan is a video monitor. This is placed where the newsman can view the news pictures on it while reading the stories which they portray.

Three Answers

The next floor plan to be considered is for a studio production exercise called *Three Answers*. This program is opened by a host who, having cited some problem or situation deserving of comment, propounds a question regarding it. With him, he explains, are three guests who will answer the question in turn. He calls on guest #1, who gives his opinion. The host comments briefly on this answer, then repeats the question for guest #2. The process is repeated with guest #3. Then the host summarizes, thanks his guests, and closes the program.

Fig. 22/4

The floor plan is shown in *Figure 22/4*. Consult it while reading the following rationale for its design.

7   First, the director establishes performer relationships.

How should the performers be arranged to support the action of the program? In this instance there are two entities to be related: the questioner and those questioned. These entities require some sort of visual separation, but since they are not in conflict there is no reason for diametrical opposition; hence the director visualizes an L-shaped relationship.

Since he desires a mood of relaxed informality, he avoids desks or tables, seating the host in an armchair and unifying the guests by placing them all on the same sofa. He chooses an angled sofa to bridge the corner between host and guests, blending them into a closer relationship.

The group needs to be as compact as possible for two reasons. First, the wider the shot needed to establish the total group, the smaller its members will be on the screen and the more difficult it will be to discern their facial expressions. Second, the wider the shot, the higher the boom microphone must be raised to keep out of the picture, and the farther it must travel to come within range of each speaker. In this respect, the present plan, while not ideal, will get by: when the microphone is centered and two feet above head level, its maximum distance from any speaker will be about 4–½ feet.

8   The director places his cameras.

Camera 2 has been angled to show the guests from as nearly full face as possible when they turn towards the host. Camera 1 has been angled to favor the host and also to take establishing shots of the group. Letters "a," "b," and "c" indicate that the camera will begin on the host only, then dolly back and simultaneously pan to the three guests, and finally reach a spot from which it can include both host and guests. By shooting the sofa from an angle to overlap the guests, it can obtain larger images of them than from the front, where they would present a wider spread.

The distance of camera from subject and the choice of camera lens are interdependent considerations. For camera 1's opening shot, the director chooses a 50mm lens because its generous depth of field will facilitate staying in focus while dollying and its relatively wide angle of view will embrace the group at a shorter distance than would be required by a lens of longer focal length. From this distance (location "c") it can frame the host's chair on an 8–½" lens when one-shots of the host are being alternated with one-shots of the guests. To make these alternating shots consistent in framing, perspective, and focal characteristics, camera 2 is placed at approximately the same distance from the guests as camera 1 is from the host, and will also take its one-shots on an 8–½" lens. From this distance it can also, if desired, include the host and guest nearest to him on a 90mm lens, or use a 50mm to include the entire group. Both cameras, then, have base locations from which they can use all their lenses to get a maximum variety of shots without moving from these locations.

9 The director considers scenery and set dressing.

The staging for *Three Answers* evinces a concern for economy, both of money and of the time needed to set and strike. Most of the background is composed of already hanging drapes. The standing pieces are all from stock, and the few there are can all be justified either for suggesting locale or for helping to achieve good pictorial composition.

Fig. 22/5

Several of the pieces serve both purposes. The wood-paneled flat suggests a contemporary interior and encourages the studio drapes to read as drapes across a broad living room window. Compositionally, as can be noted in *Figure 22/5,* the flat also serves, by backing the guests, to unite them visually and to distinguish them from the host, who is backed by the drapes.

By simulating a portion of interior wall in the shot from position "a", the 2-fold economically suggests a room. As a compositional factor, it brings the eye forward instead of letting it follow the bottom line of the drapes diagonally back and out of the picture. Similarly, in the shot from "c", the coffee table pulls the eye forward. Its mass helps to balance off the guests on the other side of the frame. It adds visual interest where there would otherwise be too much empty floor. The broad horizontal plane of its top opposes the vertical lines of the figures and helps to weigh down the composition, gravitywise, to the floor. The table also serves as a center around which the arc of the guests is curved.

Besides helping to form this arc, the angled sofa also prevents having the guests spaced with too military a regularity; note that the two men overlap, but the girl is separated from them. The still wider gap between girl and host is filled in with the vertical line of the pole lamp in the distance. All of these vertical directions are knit together by the horizontal lines of the furniture and the top of the planter.

An impression of three-dimensional space is created by the curve of the performers, the diagonal planes of walls, furniture, and bodies, and by an axis which runs from the coffee table, as the nearest element, to the pole lamp, as most prominent distant element. This impression would be further enhanced, of course, by light and shadow and by focus differentiations, which are absent in the purely linear illustration. Also missing from the illustration is the distribution of colors or of gray-scale values. Perhaps you would like to experiment with how these should be distributed.

10   Vertical relationships in the picture are influenced by the floor plan.

It is possible to leave the considerations just discussed to a scenic artist, but it is unlikely that he will achieve a perfect solution unless your floor plan shows the relationship between performer locations and camera locations. The elevations of television settings must be designed to suit the shots, complementing rather than interfering with the appearance of the performers in these shots. For example, were the pole lamp arbitrarily located, it might appear on camera directly behind a performer and seem to grow out of the top of his head. Its proper location can be determined by projecting on the floor plan a line which starts at camera 1 and passes between the host and the guest nearest to him. On this line, a short distance from the planter, is the spot where the pole lamp should be. By similar projections one can locate where the ends of the flat and the 2-fold should occur.

If you have already completed the scenery and furniture locations on your floor plan and are experimenting with camera locations for certain shots, you can use this same method of projecting lines to determine where, in a given shot, elements in the background will appear in relation to the performers in front of them. For example, using the plan for *Three Answers,* lay a ruler between camera 2 and the left end of the 6'6" flat. Where will the edge of the flat appear in camera 2's shot of the performer nearest the host—to the right or left of her head, or immediately behind it?

Microquiz

For a last example of floor planning, please identify yourself with the director of a program called *Microquiz.* A plan for this program is to be contrived from advance data supplied by its producer.

According to this data, a husband and wife will be interviewed briefly and then invited to guess the identity of pictures shown on a rear-projection screen. The projector is to be operated through remote control by the program host. Its projection lens angle requires that it be twice as far behind the screen as the screen is wide. Both host and guests must be able to see the slides. The television audience must see the slides and must see the program participants both separately and in various appropriate combinations. The shot changes are likely to be frequent. Two 3″ image orthicon cameras will be used.

What is the best interrelationship of cameras, participants, and rear projection screen?

11   There is more than one possible relationship.

From the previous floor plans shown to you, it might seem that the solution of a given planning problem will come readily to the director's mind. This is not necessarily so. He may have to think through various arrangements, possibly sketching them on paper, and evaluating each against the requirements until he hits upon the one most likely to serve. There is more than one way to shoot a show. Don't always stop with the first solution which occurs to you. There may be a better one still in your head.

For example, *Figures 22/6* through *22/9* show four possible ways to shoot *Microquiz*. Each will be analyzed in turn.

Figure 22/6

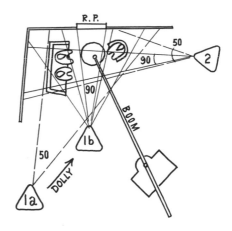

Fig. 22/6

Here, the host is in an armchair, his guests on a sofa. Camera 1 starts back where it can establish the group on a 50mm lens. For the quiz, it dollies in to where it can use the 50mm to include the host and screen, or the 90mm to pan between the host and the screen. Camera 2 is placed where its 50mm will take the total group, its 90mm the two guests, and its 8–½″ each guest separately.

What problems might arise from this arrangement? The rear

projection screen may be placed so close to the performers that its images will be diluted by spill light from the performance area. Moving it back, however, will probably require enlarging the images, which will make them less brilliant. It may be possible to restrict spill light by cross-keying, i.e., by lighting the guests from the direction of camera 2 and the host from an instrument behind the guests, so that the light beams run more or less parallel to the rear wall rather than towards it.

Audio pickup in this solution may not be satisfactory unless each performer wears a chest microphone. Otherwise, since there are no surfaces to support table microphones, it will be necessary to use a boom microphone, and for this the performers are rather too widely separated.

Figure 22/7

This is an attempt to solve the audio problem just discussed. Although the performers are in much the same relationship as before, they have been moved closer together and seated at a table, which permits the use of table microphones. To view the host as nearly full face as possible, camera 1 has been stationed close to the desk—so close, indeed, that it may disturb the concentration of the guest nearest to it.

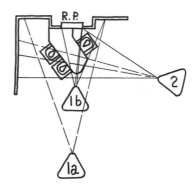

Fig. 22/7

Figure 22/8

This attempt is probably not as promising as the preceding one, since it catches the host in profile at best—although he might be given a swivel chair to facilitate turning towards camera for his opening and close. Camera 2 might be equipped with a zoom lens for zooming between close-ups of the screen and wider shots which include the performers.

Fig. 22/8

Figure 22/9

In this arrangement, audio pickup is feasible and there is less danger of light diluting the projected images since the performers have been moved to one side of the screen. Both host and guests can be shown relatively face-to, and the cameras are sufficiently distant to prevent their intruding on the performers' concentration. Unlike the two previous plans, no specially constructed table is required.

Fig. 22/9

Perhaps, then, this scheme has possibilities. Before deciding on it, however, the director tests it against a representative portion of the program action to see what kind and variety of shots it will provide.

1 (50mm) HOST OPENS STANDING AT R.P. SCREEN. AS HE WALKS TO TABLE AND SITS, PAN WITH HIM AND ESTABLISH THE COMPLETE TABLE, INCLUDING ALREADY SEATED GUESTS.

2 (8½") PAN FROM ONE GUEST TO THE OTHER AS THEY ARE INTRODUCED

1 (90mm) HOST. PAN LEFT TO SCREEN WHEN HE INTRODUCES FIRST PICTURE.

2 (90mm) BRIEF CUT-AWAY: BOTH GUESTS LOOKING TOWARDS SCREEN.

1 (90mm) SCREEN. PAN RIGHT TO HOST WHEN HE SAYS THAT TIME FOR VIEWING SLIDE IS UP.

2 (8½")   PAN GUESTS AS EACH GUESSES.

 1 (50mm) SCREEN AND HOST AS HOST TELLS CORRECT ANSWER.

 2 90mm)   BOTH GUESTS, FOR THEIR REACTIONS; THEN PAN LEFT TO HOST AS HE TURNS TOWARD SCREEN TO INTRODUCE SECOND SLIDE.

 1 (90mm) SCREEN.

 2 (50mm) ALL THREE LOOKING AT SCREEN, OFF LEFT.

 1 (90mm) HOST AS HE CALLS TIME AND ASKS FOR GUESSES.

 2 (8½")   PAN GUESTS AS EACH GUESSES.

 1 (50mm) ALL THREE, AS HOST GIVES CORRECT ANSWER

   . . . . etc.

   This test demonstrates that the set-up is capable of providing meaningful shots. And although the game follows the same routine over and over, the set-up provides a sufficient variety of shots to enliven what might otherwise prove to be a very monotonous visual sequence.

Even so, you may be able to work out an even more satisfactory solution.

At any rate, when working on floor plans, don't settle for the first solution that occurs to you. Try several until you are sure you have found the most promising.

In evaluating a plan, don't think of it merely as outlines of scenery, furniture, and camera positions. View it, rather, in terms of shot possibilities such as those sketched above. These are the end towards which your floor plan is the means. The plan is only as good as the pictures which it enables you to present to your audience.

Some Further Considerations

12 Relate your plan to studio conditions.

Most of the factors which you have been invited to consider when designing a floor plan have been concerned with communicating the meaning and action of a program to its audience. The design may be modified, however, by some considerations not connected with the program, but rather with accommodating the production to the studio where it will take place. Thus, you may need to take into account:

. . . the location and needs of other set-ups which must occupy the studio at the same time.

. . . the possibility, when doing live programming, that cameras, boom microphone, and even some of the lights used on your program will be needed on previous or following programs, with a minute or less in which to make the transfer.

. . . studio traffic patterns—the need to keep entrances and passageways clear and to provide access to your area without crossing in front of cameras or interfering with other studio activities.

. . . the location of studio outlets for camera, microphone, and video monitor cables, or for supplying utilities such as water, gas, or 220 volt electrical power to equipment used on your program.

. . . the location of overhead pipe grids, battens, and traveler curtain tracks, so that your plan does not call for scenic pieces and lighting instruments where it is not convenient to suspend them.

. . . the possible desirability of being able to view both your performance area and camera deployment area through the window of the control room.

13   Try to economize time and money.

When planning your set-up, minimize setting and striking time where possible by using already hung pieces such as drapes and cycloramas. Minimize construction by using stock pieces when feasible. Condense as much as possible the area to be backed by scenery and lighted. Restrict technical operations, scenic embellishments, and special effects to whatever can be accomplished during the allowed preparation time. Submit your plans to the technical departments early enough to be carried out during their normal production schedule. Provide all of the information needed by these departments so that time will not be lost through guesswork or the need to seek you out for further details. Avoid last-minute revisions.

14   In summary, the satisfactory floor plan should:

(1) Establish meaningful physical relationships between the performers, and between them and whatever properties and scenic elements may be engaged in the action.

(2) Provide for performers' movements that are meaningful, animated, and convincing.

(3) Insure that shots are so alternated between cameras that each camera can show what is expected of it.

(4) Locate the cameras to get each shot with the proper angle and framing.

(5) Prevent camera delays due to unncesssary lens changes and camera repositioning.

(6) Permit effective lighting, with no undesirable shadows.

(7) Permit good audio pickup.

(8) Allow the available technical crew to function effectively.

(9) Locate furniture and scenic elements where they will support and enhance the pictorial composition of each intended shot.

(10) Relate to conditions in the studio to be used.

(11) Reflect a concern for economy of money and manpower.

By governing where your subjects and cameras will stand and move, the floor plan determines to a large extent what shots you can get and how these shots will look. But the floor plan in turn should be determined by what shots you want to get and how you want them to look. Hence, a great deal of what you learn about television picture-making—not only from what you have read here, but also from your future reading and thinking and experience—will ultimately be reflected in your floor plans.

Chapter 23

Efficiency

Although you may have designed superbly communicative television pictures, you have to rely on others for their realization. The performers, the service departments which assemble your production materials and facilities, the studio and control room crews which operate the facilities—all must be oriented to their objectives and guided in the achievement of them, each separate contribution being coordinated with all of the others to make a perfect whole. And this perfection must be achieved with due regard to always existing limitations of time and resources.

The realization of your pictures, therefore, depends on how well you direct the activities of people and make the most of the limitations within which they work. It depends upon your qualities as an administrator and efficiency expert.

This chapter traces the course through which your efficiency must operate, from the initial conception of your production through the facilities rehearsal. To promote efficiency, it asks you to observe certain practices, the first of which is:

1   Work closely with the service departments.

1.1   Give them sufficient time and information to do a job which will reflect credit on them and on you.

As soon as you know your program objectives and how you propose to accomplish them, you will need to supply various kinds of information to the departments which will carry out your production requirements. If your program is a new and reasonably important venture, it would be advisable to hold a production conference involving, besides yourself, the producer and client's representative (if any), and representatives of staging, lighting, engineering, art, and any other department which will contribute to the production. This conference provides an opportunity to:

. . . Arrive at a mutual understanding of the production purpose, format, and style.

. . . Determine the facilities needed and the time and space in studio required.

. . . Schedule dates and times for rehearsals and actual broadcast or taping sessions.

. . . Discuss the budget and desirable modifications in it.

. . . Iron out any disagreements or technical difficulties.

Whether or not a general conference is held, you can profitably hold individual conferences with members of the various departments to work out the specifications for everything you require. To confirm and record these requirements, you should use the prescribed forms for submitting floor plans of your setting, ordering titles and other graphics, clearing music, and obtaining various other materials and services.

Films, slides, and other materials which you may procure from sources outside the station will need to be in the hands of appropriate station personnel by prescribed times. There will also be a deadline for your script or program rundown. If there is a standard format for these, it is to your advantage to follow it, since the operators on your program will be familiar with this format and can therefore follow it with minimum chance for error. There also may be required a cover sheet listing properties, music and sound effects, and the films and slides to be projected. Such lists allow operators to check whether the items are all on hand and to have them arranged in the proper order.

1.2   To increase the possibilities of getting the services you need:

Meet the deadlines of the service departments. Remember that your program is not the only one on their assembly line.

Be certain that all responsibilities are allocated. Let there be no occasion to say, "I thought *you* were going to do that!"

Anticipate and provide for everything. If you need a tractor in the setting, will it fit through the studio door? Can the ice cream be kept refrigerated? Is there a 220v. outlet for operating the clothes dryer? How long will it take to light the glossy automobile? Will you be allowed by fire regulations to start its motor in the studio?

If you contemplate any unusual effects, check with experts regarding their feasibility and test them well before camera rehearsal.

Take nothing for granted. Check the progress of preparation and procurement. Be sure that everything is going to be ready and to conform to specifications.

2 Save studio time by advance preparation.

Come to the studio with as much of the production organized as possible, knowing exactly what remains to be done and how you are going to do it. Studio time is too precious to use for determining what the performers will do and say or what kind of shots the director will take.

Except in the case of routine and extremely simple programs, work with your performers outside of the studio, rehearsing in a mockup of the setting and checking your shots with a viewing device. Establish the timing of the performance, including an estimated allowance for fades, dissolves, musical bridges, and other transitional material.

For personnel not present at these outside rehearsals, it is sometimes expedient to prepare written instructions in order to minimize the time taken by verbal instructions during studio rehearsal. Besides shot plots for the cameramen, one can write out cues and instructions for other operators such as the audio engineer, curtain puller, or lighting control man. One can also include directions in the booth announcer's script: "Pause until camera has dollied in . . . Wait for next painting to show on monitor," etc.

3 In studio, accomplish as much as you can before the cameras are ready.

For example, you may be able to:

. . . Check the scenery and lighting set-up.

. . . See that the projectionist has film and slides readied in the proper sequence.

. . . See that the audio operator knows his cues and has located the proper starting places on records and audio tapes.

. . . Check the placement of properties and easel cards.

. . . Work with the floor crew on manual operations such as the flipping of easel pictures.

. . . Work with the performers to accustom them to studio conditions, relating their business and action to the actual furniture and scenery, solving their problems with the wearing of chest microphones, etc.

. . . See that the floor manager and the performers have a mutual understanding about the meaning of the floor manager's signals and when they are to occur.

. . . Set levels for the various audio channels.

. . . If time permits, hold a complete dry rehearsal of dialogue and action. Sometimes it may be possible to have the cameramen watch this before they man their cameras.

4   Assuming that you have some camera rehearsal, make the most of it.

Ideally, for perfecting any new production which involves considerable movement by performers and cameras, there should be enough camera rehearsal time to allow a continuous run-through. This will give both talent and technicians practice in sustaining a coordinated performance and will allow a final check on total running time. Following this run-through, there should be a sufficient interval before broadcast or recording to make last-minute corrections, restore various items to their starting positions, and re-balance the cameras.

Before the run-through there should be a stop-and-start or blocking rehearsal to set each major shot and transition, taking them sequentially, one by one. It is to this blocking rehearsal that the following suggestions apply.

4.1   Save time.

Start the rehearsal punctually.

Know precisely what you want to do and move briskly along from one objective to another. Your plans should be definite but flexible. If a camera has to be worked on, be ready to do something which mainly involves the still serviceable cameras, or work on a performer's interpretation, or an audio effect, etc.

By thorough advance preparation you should have forestalled the need for any major changes. Just one change may entail many others. Changing the boom position may necessitate re-lighting. Re-lighting may entail moving the furniture and performers out of the way. Meanwhile the clock keeps ticking.

Make your instructions precise and phrase them in terms of action. To a performer, for instance: "Lou, first look towards the map. Now move— that's it, clear across to Maine. Now stop and point. Good!" Or to a cameraman: "Bill, you need to get in more quickly, and into a tighter shot; all we want is the keyboard, not the whole accordion. Ready? Go! In . . . in . . . tilt down more, and in . . . in . . . and stop! That's the idea. Let's try it once more now to smooth out the jerky tilting." (Note that Bill is told the objective of his dolly-in. Compliance can be speeded up when a person comprehends what is to be done, and why.)

There's usually no need in a blocking rehearsal for performers to run through all their dialogue. If the shot doesn't change, interrupt them and move on to the next change.

On the other hand, do involve the performers whenever their movement or dialogue affects the shots you are setting up. Thus, obviously, the performer must rise and walk if you are to perfect the tilting up and panning with him. Less obviously, perhaps, the duration of a speech may affect a pictorial transition: what the master of ceremonies says to introduce the panelists may determine the amount of time a camera has in which to dolly back and pan to the panel.

As mentioned previously in this book, you can sometimes expedite matters by working part of the time on the studio floor in direct communication with the performers. Also as previously mentioned, you should proportion your time so that overconcern with one problem does not rob time from others of equal importance.

Your job is to keep everything going. You cannot do this if you lose yourself in concerns which others can handle for you. Delegate authority, so that you have lieutenants working on several concerns at the same time. Identify those things which others can be working on while you're busy rehearsing something else. Get these things started early in the rehearsal so they'll be ready by the time you need to weave them into the show.

5   Your watchwords are STOP, LOOK, AND LISTEN—not FAITH, HOPE, AND CHARITY.

—well, charity, maybe, but not the other two. Never take anything on faith and hope that it will work. Demand to see and listen to it. Only thus will you be sure that people understand what you want and are capable of achieving it. And before the actual performance, check to see that everything used in rehearsal has been restored to its proper starting position and is ready to go.

Throughout rehearsal, look and listen critically. Remember what was said in the chapter on "Concealing Mechanics" about professionalism being, in the main, a painstaking attention to details.

On the other hand, there are times when it doesn't pay to stop and correct every small mistake. If rehearsal time is short, come to it knowing which things are the most critical or difficult, and restrict your attention to them. Furthermore, constant stopping can become discouraging and irritating to your personnel. It is often more important to give them the feel of the whole, to let them practice sustaining the continuity of the performance, than to get lost among the pieces and never put them together.

When you do discuss problems with a person, don't point out too many problems in the same breath—unless you want to overwhelm him, confuse him, discourage him, and have him forget most of them.

6   Maintain the morale of your team.

6.1   You are their servant as well as their boss.

Give them the information they need when they need it. Restrict your demands to what they and their equipment can reasonably accomplish.

6.2   Show them that you respect their abilities.

Give them a chance to exercise these abilities. Make clear what is needed, but don't try to do their job for them. Keep yourself open to their suggestions—without, of course, letting anarchy set in. Find a way to recognize their contributions without cheapening your praise through overspending it. Make them feel that it's their show, too.

6.3   Beware of exploiting your own ego.

Crew people tend to resent the director who always uses the first person pronoun: "Give *me* a closeup of so and so," or, *"I* want to see your eight-inch lens." People on the studio floor tend to resent the unseen presence who dominates them over the studio address system without giving them an opportunity to discuss their problems with him face to face.

6.4   Control yourself.

Never use the intercommunication system to publicly disparage an individual. Make every effort to stay calm and collected and to set an example of confidence. Anxiety is contagious; don't spread it.

6.5   Remember that idleness breeds restlessness and apprehension.

Be considerate of people's time. If, through unforeseen difficulties, they must be kept waiting, explain the situation briefly to them and give them a break, asking them to return to the studio at a certain time when you know you'll be able to work with them.

Much more might be said about the technique of supervision, but perhaps you have read enough to realize your need to become proficient at it. Your ability to design effective television pictures will count for little unless you can get your performers and technicians to bring those pictures to life on the screen.

Chapter 24

Calling the Shots

During most television performances the director calls the shots—gives the verbal directions which regulate what the technicians do and when they do it.

There are exceptions, mainly in the larger studios. In some instances the technical director may cue the cameramen, following a shot plan established by the director in rehearsal. Or an assistant director may get the cameras ready for their shots, with the director calling for the shots to be switched and guiding the cameras while they are feeding the program. Lighting cues may be delegated to the lighting director, and audio cues to the audio director. When programs have been fully scripted and camera plotted, the cameramen and other technicians may follow written instructions with a minimum of verbal cueing from the control room.

But every director on his way up is likely to work where his verbal instructions will coordinate the work of many persons: cameramen, boom operator, audio control operator, floor manager, booth announcer, projectionist, video tape operator, and switcher among them. Even when he does his own switching, the director may be expected to call the takes so that all technicians will know what picture changes are occurring without needing to keep their eyes glued to a monitor.

Therefore, if you have not already done so, you will need to become proficient at shot calling—so proficient, indeed, that you can relegate the routine aspects of it to your subconscious, as with typing, bicycling, or driving a car, to free your attention for the thoughtful and creative aspects. Although you can reach this stage only through actual and repeated practice, the following pointers may help to guide and speed your learning.

1   Take it easy and learn by degrees.

You might start with a short, easily improvised sequence in which a host asks a guest one question:

CHEST SHOT, HOST	HOST:	INTRODUCES SELF AND PRO-GRAM. HE HAS A GUEST TO QUESTION. ASKS QUESTION.
DOLLY BACK TO 2-SHOT		
CHEST SHOT, GUEST	GUEST:	ANSWERS.
CHEST SHOT, HOST	HOST:	COMMENTS ON ANSWER, CLOSES PROGRAM.

If you have never called shots before, begin by just seeing whether you can fade a camera in and out on the host, without even having him say anything. Don't worry too much at this stage about memorizing the correct terminology for your directions. It's more important to think about what, at each stage, you have to get done:

Think this:	*. . . and therefore say:*
I must alert people that we're about to begin.	STAND BY.
The switcher must pre-set his fader bank to come up on the proper camera.	READY TO FADE UP ONE.
Now, have him come up on it.	FADE UP ONE.
That's all, so ready the switcher to end the show.	READY TO FADE TO BLACK.
Have him do it.	FADE TO BLACK.

Next, try repeating the same thing, but having the host speak his introduction. For this, in addition to what you did before, you need to (1) get the microphone opened, and (2) have your floor manager cue the host that he's coming on camera and microphone. And in order to end the show, you'll need to know in advance the last words the host plans to say.

Think this:	*. . . and therefore say:*
Alert everyone.	STAND BY.
Ready the switcher.	READY TO FADE UP ONE.
The audience must hear the host.	OPEN MIKE.
Alert the host that the camera's coming on.	CUE HIM.
Now he's ready to have his picture taken.	FADE UP ONE.
The show will end when he finishes speaking, so ready the switcher.	READY TO FADE TO BLACK.
(Listening) He's ending his speech.	FADE TO BLACK.

When you've mastered this, add the dolly-back which brings the guest into view. Start the dolly when the host mentions having a guest with him and go to black as soon as the dolly is completed. To avoid a wait at the end, ready the switcher for the fade-out while the camera is still dollying.

Your directions will be the same as before until after you've said, "Fade up one." Then:

Think this:	*. . . and therefore say:*
He's going to mention the guest.	READY TO DOLLY BACK.
He's starting to mention him.	DOLLY BACK.
The end's coming up.	READY TO FADE TO BLACK.
(Watching monitor) The camera's back far enough.	HOLD THE DOLLY.
That's all.	FADE TO BLACK.

Finally, you'll be able to add the second camera, taking it when the guest begins to speak. Then you'll take back to the first camera for the host's conclusion. Since this camera has dollied back into a two-shot, however, you will have to get it changed to a longer lens while camera 2 is on, so that it can get its closing one-shot of the host. The whole sequence, then, will go something like this:

Think this:	*. . . and therefore say:*
I must have the cameras ready.	OPENING SHOTS, PLEASE . . . 1, CHEST SHOT OF THE HOST AND READY TO DOLLY BACK . . . 2, CHEST SHOT OF THE GUEST.
(Watching monitors) That doesn't look quite right.	2, A LITTLE MORE HEADROOM, PLEASE.
(Watching clock) It's almost starting time. Ready the switcher.	STAND BY. READY TO FADE UP 1.
Audience must hear.	OPEN MIKE
Alert the host.	CUE HIM.
Show the host as he starts to talk.	FADE UP 1.
Guest's coming up soon.	READY TO DOLLY BACK.
(Listening) Host is starting to mention guest.	DOLLY BACK.
(Looking) Is 2's shot of the guest still OK? 1 has dollied far enough.	HOLD THE DOLLY.
(Listening and watching) Guest's about to speak.	TAKE 2.
1's just off his shot. What's his next shot?	1, ON YOUR SHOULDER SHOT OF THE HOST.
(Listening) Guest's finished his answer.	TAKE 1.
End's coming soon.	READY TO FADE TO BLACK.
(Watching and listening) Host is finished, verbally and visually.	FADE TO BLACK

Once you've been able to do all this, you're well on your way. If it seems complicated at first, remember that with practice it will get to be second nature to you. Most of it will roll out of you without your consciously thinking about it.

2 Shot calling is not reading words off a script.

Some beginners write what they're supposed to say and then try to read it aloud during the performance. This rarely works. If you lose your place on the page, you probably won't know what is supposed to happen next. Even if you do manage to follow along the page, you won't know what is happening to the program since you aren't looking at the pictures or listening to the sounds or feeling with your sense of timing when the changes should occur.

Directors usually do mark their scripts with symbols or brief reminders which tell them at a glance what's coming next. But these should be only reminders. Mainly, you should know what's supposed to be happening, following a thought sequence like that in the "Think this" columns above. Start by grasping the overall pattern of events—for example: "Host first . . . dolly back to include guest . . . guest alone . . . then host alone." With this in mind, you'll likely find that during the performance, if you really watch and listen to what's going on, each present occurrence will remind you of what's to follow it. Seeing the host, you'll remember that he has a guest with him whom you'll have to include by dollying back. Dollying back to include the guest will remind you that next the guest gets a shot to himself. Listening to the guest's answer will remind you that the host will comment on that answer—and so on.

And as you watch and listen, you'll also be able to do the other things: see that the next shot is properly set up, see that the present shot looks right, refer occasionally to the clock, evaluate the quality and volume of the audio, sense the pace at which to guide a pan or dolly or dissolve and the time at which to call a take or cue in music.

Remember, then: calling directions is not just reading, or even speaking. It's thinking, feeling, watching, and listening.

3 Make your directions brief and to the point.

Say: "1 on the girl"—not: "Camera 1, please change your lens and get ready for the shot of the girl."

Unnecessary words can make an instruction less intelligible. They waste time which the technician needs for getting ready to do what you want him to do, and which you need for giving other directions at times when the cues come thick and fast. They also communicate less urgency than is needed to keep a crew on its toes.

4   Use the vocabulary of your particular station.

Terminology is not completely standardized throughout the country. Be sure that your terminology is understood at the station where you report for work. Highly original phrases may not be understood, or understood as quickly as they need to be. Nevertheless, personnel at most stations should understand such variants as:

Dolly back—Pull back
Ready music—Standby music
Music in—Hit music
Fade in 2—Fade up 2—Fade 2
Fade to black—Go to black
Tilt up—pan up
etc.

5   Know when to give ready or standby cues.

These are normally given in the following circumstances:

5.1   Before air time to alert everyone for the start of the program.

The floor manager will relay this cue to persons in the studio without earphones.

5.2   To any operator who has been out of action for some time, including:

. . . The booth announcer, who, usually having nothing to do on the program for some time after his opening announcement, may lose himself in other concerns.
. . . The projectionist, before a series of slide changes or a film sequence in which he plays a part. He may be across the room, rewinding film or setting up slides in another projector.
. . . A cameraman who has not been used for the past several shots.
. . . The audio operator, for opening a microphone. Although he may have been involved constantly in riding gain, opening a new microphone is a different operation which may not be a part of his present thought pattern.

5.3   For any operation which requires some preparatory action— thus:

Before playing a disc recording, the operator must have the stylus in the proper groove, the turntable motor on, one hand on the disc and the other on the volume control.

Before dollying a pedestal or tripod, the cameraman must have his wheels lined up in the desired direction and be ready to push or pull as the case may be.

Before making a dissolve, super, or fade, the switcher must pre-set a camera on the opposite fader bank and have his hands on the fader levers.

5.4   To conform with the particular practice of your station.

Some stations, for example, require ready cues before camera takes. Where image retention (burn-in) is a problem, this lets a cameraman keep his camera in motion until just before his shot is needed. And during improvised action shot by three or more cameras, it identifies which of the idle cameras is to be used next. On the other hand, during a brisk alternation of shots, it is difficult to include ready cues and still take the shots on time.

6   Practice starting your cues to finish at the necessary time.

Commands for takes should finish a fraction of a second before the takes are wanted in order to allow for the switcher's reaction time.

Film must be rolled before it can be switched into the program. After starting, older models of film projectors may require several seconds to get up to proper speed. When these are used for film inserts, the cue to roll them may need to be given as early as two sentences before speech from the studio is to cease. The director should know what these final sentences are to be and remind the performer to deliver them verbatim so that, recognizing them, the director can give the roll cue at the necessary time.

7   Several cues may be needed simultaneously.

Sometimes a number of operations may coincide or follow one another so swiftly that the director has no time to deliver all the cues for them in their standard form.

Getting to studio from opening titles over which music has been played would theoretically require you to say, "Music out, open boom mike, cue talent, dissolve to 2." This can be condensed to, "Mike, cue, dissolve." (In this instance, the audio operator understands that he is to take music out when the dissolve occurs.) In any situation where several cues would make too much of a mouthful, you can arrange in advance for each operator to act on a single cue from you, such as the word "dissolve."

There may be some operations which, by custom at your station, you will not have to cue at all. For example, the audio operator may be expected to automatically close the studio microphones whenever the program moves to some other source of sound (such as sound on film) which requires no audio from the studio.

8   There is a preferable sequence for some sets of cues.

When a turntable takes longer to get up to speed than the switcher does to fade up the opening picture, give the music cue before the fade cue. It is customary to say, "Music, fade in one," rather than, "Fade in one, music."

Also say, "Mike, cue, dissolve" when going to a performer at the start of a studio sequence. Do not say, "Dissolve, mike, cue." To bring the camera up on him before his microphone has been opened may miss his starting word if he takes his cue from the tally light instead of from the floor manager. Do not say, "Mike, dissolve, cue." To bring the camera up on him before he has been cued is liable to catch him in the process of taking his cue from the floor manager. Therefore, say, "Mike, cue, dissolve."

9   Follow these suggestions for giving directions to cameramen:

As soon as a camera goes off the air, specify its next shot. Make it habitual to think, "It's off; what does it do next?" Thus, your directions will run: "Take 1; 2 closeup on the bowl . . . Take 2; 1 hold your shot . . . Take 1; 2 on a cover shot . . ." etc.

In addressing the off-air camera, give its number before stating what it is to do. Thus: "2, pan over to the mayor." There are two reasons for this precaution: (1) If you do not start with the number, the cameraman who is on the air may assume that the direction is for him—panning to the mayor, for example, off his present subject. (2) When more than one camera is off the air, their operators, if obliged to wait in order to learn which of them you are addressing, will lose time which should have gone to carrying out the instruction.

When setting up shots of people, you are likely to get more accurate framing if you ask for a "shoulder shot" or "waist shot" rather than a "closeup" or "medium shot."

Before citing the area to be framed, you may need to specify what lens is to be used. For example, the cameraman can get a waist shot either by changing to a longer lens or by dollying closer to the subject. If he dollies in, he may end too close for the cover shot which you want from him next.

So you say, "1 on your 135 for a waist shot of Carla." On the other hand, the next thing you want may be a dolly back from the subject. Since the cameraman cannot dolly acceptably on a 135mm lens, you tell him in this instance, "1, push in for a waist shot of Carla on your present lens." The choice of lens also affects the perspective of your pictures and helps to determine which subjects are sharply and which softly focused. Since these are matters which affect the purpose of your communication, they should be under your control.

How much verbal information you give the cameramen about setting up their shots will depend upon how much they already know about their assignment. To the degree that they have been thoroughly rehearsed, you will need to be less explanatory. If they have shot sheets taped to their cameras, you may simply refer to the shots by their numbers: "2, ready with shot 6," etc.

As explained in the chapter on "Keeping Up With the Action," make it clear to the cameraman in advance when you wish them to find shots for you and when you wish them to wait for your instructions. When they are finding shots for you, keep your eyes on the monitors and give them your reaction to whatever they are offering you.

10   The tone and tempo of your directions will influence the crew's responses.

By the tone and tempo of your directions you can communicate a feeling of snappy efficiency, or easy relaxation, or some other desired psychological set. How you speak can be used to guide the pace and rhythm of a dolly or pan, regulate the speed of a dissolve, control the crescendo and diminuendo of music, or make a take occur at the proper moment. When guiding operators who are in the control room with you, such as the switcher and the audio operator, you may wish to occasionally supplement your voice with the snap of a finger or the movement of an arm such as an orchestra conductor might employ—provided, however, that these are helpful and are not done merely to dramatize your role.

11   Study the following example of cues for a complete short program.

Commands of execution are in underlined capital letters. Preparatory commands are indented and in lower case.

As previously mentioned, terminology varies between one station and another and between one director and another. You are not being asked to adopt the following phraseology word for word, but rather to understand its general style and purpose:

DIRECTIONS	SCRIPT	
Opening shots, please. Ready music, ready to fade up 1. MUSIC—FADE UP 1.	TITLE (on drum)	MUSIC: THEME UP & UNDER BOOTH ANNCR:

MUSIC UNDER—AN-NOUNCE.
  Ready boom mike.
  Ready to dissolve to 2.
		From the Flagstaff Museum it's Bob Daniels with . . . Nature Quiz!
		MUSIC: OUT

MIKE, CUE, DISSOLVE. Ready to dissolve to 7 for film with sound on.	MS BOB	BOB: INTRODUCTORY RE-MARKS, DISCUSS PENGUINS, ENDING:
ROLL FILM.		And now let's watch some penguins in their native habitat.

DISSOLVE TO 7, SOUND ON.
  2, we'll be dissolving back to you on a long shot of Bob. Be ready to pan him to the guest . . . 1, get a closeup of the mystery object . . . Ready to dissolve to 2. Film ends in 10 seconds—stand by . . .
MIKE, CUE, DISSOLVE.
2, PAN WITH HIM—GOOD!
	FILM
	(3:16)
	
	LS BOB
	PAN
	WITH HIM
	TO GUEST
		SOUND ON FILM
		
		    BOB:
		
		EXPLAIN QUIZ. MENTION GUEST & WALK OVER TO CHAT WITH HIM BRIEFLY. THEN:

1 steady . . .
TAKE 1.
  2, dolly in on guest. Ready to super 8.
SUPER 8.
  Ready to lose super. Then we'll be taking 2 quickly.
	CU MYS-TERY OB-JECT
	SUPER
	SLIDE
	 (name of object)
		Now let's see if you know what this is. (AD LIB) . . . and meanwhile we'll let the audience in on the secret . . . Are you ready to guess?

LOSE SUPER, TAKE 2.
  Change slide on 8.
2, DOLLY BACK TO IN-CLUDE BOB.
  1 on closing titles.
	CU GUEST
	
	BOB &
	GUEST
		GUEST:
		GIVES HIS ANSWER.
		BOB:
		AWARDS NATURE CLUB POINTS.
		THANKS GUEST.

2, PAN WITH HIM. Ready to dissolve to 8.	PAN BOB INTO 1-SHOT	MOVES AWAY, BACK TO HIS OPENING STATION. EXPLAINS HOW AUDIENCE CAN SUBMIT QUESTIONS . . .

DISSOLVE TO 8.
  Ready music. Ready to dis-solve to 2.
LAP SLIDE.
MUSIC UNDER.
DISSOLVE TO 2.
  Ready to dissolve to 1.
  Ready to roll titles.
	SLIDE
	(Address)
	SLIDE
	
	(Name)
	
	BOB
		Write to this address . . .
		(READ IT) . . . and be sure to include your name.
		MUSIC: THEME IN UNDER
		BOB:
		
		DISCUSS NEXT SHOW, ENDING:
		See you then on . . .

DISSOLVE TO 1—MUSIC UP.
  Booth announcer,
  stand by . . .
ROLL DRUM, MUSIC UN-DER, AND ANNOUNCE.
  Ready to go to black.
	TITLE
	(on drum)
		Nature Quiz!
		MUSIC: UP, THEN UNDER FOR:
		  BOOTH ANNCR:

	MUSEUM CREDIT (on drum) DANIELS CREDIT (on drum)	Nature Quiz is written and produced for the Flagstaff Museum by Bob Daniels.
ROLL DRUM. MUSIC UP. GO TO BLACK.		MUSIC: UP TO TIME.

APPENDIX

As mentioned in the Introduction, this book was compiled from handouts issued to television directing classes. With one exception these handouts could be classified either as Principles or as Accessory Aptitudes. The one which could not is offered here as an adjunct which many students seemed to find useful.

SELECTING LENSES

Here are some of the factors which you may need to consider when selecting lenses for a given shot:

Framing

The area included in the frame depends on:

(*1*) *The focal length of the lens:* The longer the focal length, the narrower the angle, the less the area included, but the bigger your subject on the screen. And (vice versa) the shorter the focal length, the wider the angle, the more area included, but the smaller your subjects are on the screen.

(*2*) *The distance between camera and subject:* The shorter this distance, the less area included, but the bigger your subjects are on the screen. The greater the distance, the more area included, but the smaller your subjects are on the screen.

So you can frame your subject at the same size either by using a short lens with the camera close, or a long lens with the camera farther away. Which of these solutions you choose depends on:

Physical limitations: Are your cameras confined to a distant location—across the street or way back in the bleachers? Then obviously you must use the longer lenses. Is the studio so small that you can't place the camera very far from the action? Then you must favor the shorter lenses. When you can back the camera up, do you risk shooting unwanted subjects such as the boom, other cameras, or area outside the setting? Then you should move the camera closer and use shorter lenses.

Keeping up with the action: Can you use all your lenses effectively from the distance at which you have placed the camera—or must you move it between shots, thus risking a possible delay?

Avoiding disturbances: Will the camera be so close to the subject that it will bump into furniture in the set?—or disturb the performers' concentration?—or get into another camera's shot?—or throw camera shadow on the subject?—or feed blower noise or other operational noise into the microphone?

Size of closeup desired: Although closeups are commonly associated with the longer lenses, the biggest possible closeup of a tiny subject can be taken by an extreme wide-angle lens, since the subject can be focused very close to this lens. At such proximity, however, depth of field is very shallow and perspective distortion is pronounced; hence only very flat and shallow subjects can be shot in this manner.

Perspective

When two subjects are at different distances from camera, the difference in screen size between them can be increased by using a shorter lens with the camera in close. In *Figure A/1,* A is twice as close to camera as B; hence he will be twice as large as B on the screen.

Vice versa, the difference can be evened out by using a longer lens, farther from the subjects. In *Figure A/2,* A is four fifths of the distance to B and will consequently be only one fifth larger than B on the screen.

Which of these two extremes you use depends on your purpose.

Fig. A/1

Fig. A/2

Use a short (wide-angle) lens to:

 . . . Distort a face for a comic or grotesque effect.

 . . . Accentuate the force of a movement towards camera. This makes the subject enlarge rapidly and seem to cover the distance swiftly.

 . . . Add more dominance to a foreground figure in relation to one farther away. The difference in screen height between the two figures can be increased by using a low camera position.

 . . . Add variety of size and height to your pictorial composition.

 . . . Give the illusion of greater depth to your subject or to the setting.

 . . . Bring miniature subjects or scenery in the foreground into apparent scale with an actual figure in the background.

Use a long (narrow-angle) lens to:

 . . . Equalize the importance of two subjects at different distances from camera.

 . . . Make the appearance or action of the distant figure more apparent (e.g., when shooting past the catcher to the pitcher in a baseball game).

 . . . Give a feeling of compression (e.g., to make a row of tenement houses seem very crowded together or a traffic jam even more congested than it is).

When a long and a short lens both frame the same width at the plane of the performer, the short lens will include more background because of its wider angle. Therefore, if your background is too low or too narrow, or if backlights are causing halation at the top of your picture, try using a longer lens.

When both lenses show the same foreground framing, a short lens will see farther behind obstructions than a long lens. Do you want to uncover the heads of panelists who are arranged one behind another? Note how the short lens does this in *Figure A/3*.

Short Lens — Long Lens

Fig. A/3

Focus

Depth of field can be increased by using a lens of shorter focal length (if the camera remains at the same distance from the subject as with the longer lens previously used).

Both extended and limited depth of field have advantages.

Extended depth of field keeps foreground and background subjects in equally sharp focus at the same time. It makes following focus easier during advancing or receding movements either by the camera or by the subject.

Limited depth of field can be used to place more emphasis on the subject than on the background. It can be used to soften a background which is too "busy," or has imperfections such as cracks between flats or painted-looking stippling, or needs to look like sky rather than cloth.

Vertical Angle

The closer the camera, the more steeply it must tilt to frame a subject that is lower or higher than the lens. This consideration is important when the camera is mounted at a fixed height, as on a tripod.

Do you want to avoid seeing too much of a seated performer's pate or a standing performer's chin? Use a longer lens so that you can pull the camera back and shoot at a more gradual incline.

Do you want to look down to reveal the contents of a bowl? Use a short lens, in close.

Space-Time Factors

The wider the lens, the more quickly you can dolly from long shot to closeup, or vice versa. There are two reasons for this. Because depth of field is greater, it is easy to maintain focus while moving briskly. Because of the wide angle, the camera can take a full shot of the subject at a closer distance; therefore, there is less distance for it to cover when dollying in for a closeup.

The wider the lens, the more quickly you can dolly back with an advancing performer. Example: You take a one-shot of an entering character, then pull back as he advances to join another person already on the set.

Location of Items on the Floor Plan

Fig. A/4

Example 1 (see Figure A/4): The camera is to pan with a performer who moves from behind a desk to a display panel which is perpendicular to the desk. It is desired to maintain a hip shot during the entire move and end with the camera facing the panel squarely. This cannot be achieved with the long lens.

Example 2 (see Figure A/5): A performer moves to a chair and sits, the camera arcing with him to maintain him in a two-shot with his companion. On a short lens the arc is of limited distance and can be traversed quickly enough to keep up with the performer's action. On a long lens the camera would still be arcing long after he had sat down.

Fig. A/5

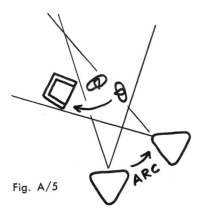

INDEX